CAIRO AND THE NILE TRAVEL GUIDE

The Ultimate Guide To Exploring Top Attractions and Activities in Cairo and the Nile with 7 days Itinerary(2023 Travel Guide)

Geneva Walker

CONTENTS

Nile?

MY CAIRO AND THE NILE TRAVEL STORY

I t was a hot summer morning when I first set foot in the magnificent metropolis of Cairo. The sun, a blazing ball in the sky, shed warm and colorful rays onto the old sandstones as if saluting the land's tenacious spirit that has stood the test of time. This was the start of an incredible voyage that captivated me with its rich tapestry of history and culture and its natural beauty. This is the start of My Cairo and Nile Travel Story.

The lofty minarets and magnificent mosques in the city center murmured stories of days gone by when mystics and academics strolled the tiny lanes in search of holy truth. These murmurs were for me and everyone who had the wonderful opportunity to visit this amazing city. The inhabitants of Cairo greeted me with open arms and piqued my interest with stories of the pharaohs, Tutankhamun's mythical wealth, and the spectacular temples constructed by their forefathers.

Cairo, a city where the old and contemporary coexist, brought me to the convoluted maze of Khan el-Khalili Bazaar. I found the pure essence of Egyptian beauty and artistry here. The souk was filled with the vivid colors of fabrics, the perfume of exotic spices, and the subtle ringing of metalworkers producing their creations. As I became a part of this throbbing blend of history and culture, my heart filled with a feeling of belonging.

The beautiful Nile River, Egypt's lifeblood, was, nonetheless, the highlight of my trip. The river flowed with mysterious elegance, nurturing the ground with its rich silt and powering the city's heart. I took a felucca ride, a classic wooden sailboat, and sailed down the river, taking in the calm of the setting sun. The warm colors of the sky swirled over the lake, producing a hypnotic tapestry of colors as memorable as the Pyramids of Giza itself.

My time in Cairo was a great eye-opener, allowing me to form stronger connections with individuals from all walks of life. The city and its people lavished me with kindness and compassion that cut beyond linguistic and cultural barriers. They led me across the city, offering their favorite hidden treasures and giving advice that resonated with my spirit.

As I go further into My Cairo and the Nile Travel Story, I will provide a realistic picture of my experiences so that you may bask in the splendor and magic of this amazing city. I shall describe my investigation of its many monuments, magical atmosphere, wonderful food, and the appeal of the Nile River as it flows through the veins of Egypt's heart. Hold on tight, my reader, as I transport you across the sands of time to a world where the echoes of the past coexist with the melodies of the present.

WELCOME TO CAIRO AND THE NILE

C airo, a huge city with a history dating back thousands of years, has long served as a gateway to some of the world's most recognizable attractions. The Nile, the world's longest river, passes across Egypt, providing unrivaled natural beauty and cultural treasures. This book will take you on an extraordinary tour, highlighting the finest of Cairo and the Nile in 2023.

Cairo's Eternal Allure

Cairo, the never-sleeping metropolis, is home to some of the world's most recognizable monuments. We must discuss Cairo by mentioning the Giza Plateau, where the towering Pyramids and Sphinx have remained for millennia, acting as a tribute to ancient Egypt's majesty. Visit the biggest of the three pyramids, the Pyramid of Khufu, followed by the smaller Pyramid of Khafre and Menkaure. Explore the neighboring Solar Boat Museum and marvel at the Sphinx, a mystery that guards the desert's secrets.

A stroll around Cairo's bustling streets is the finest way to appreciate its combination of old and contemporary. Visit Islamic Cairo, where the Al-Azhar Mosque invites travelers from all over the globe with its beautiful geometric decorations. Exploring the Citadel of Saladin, a fortified oasis that has remained for centuries, sustaining

3

the city throughout its ever-changing history, is a must. The Muhammad Ali Mosque within the Citadel, with its renowned twin minarets, offers panoramic views of Cairo's metropolis.

Visit the busy Khan el-Khalili Bazaar for a true Egyptian experience. Explore the small alleyways packed with brightly colored stores offering everything from spices, fabrics, and delicate jewelry to souvenirs and traditional handicrafts. Remember to visit one of the numerous coffee shops, such as the famed El Fishawy, where you may enjoy traditional mint tea or sample a shisha while listening to lively discussions.

A Trip Down The Nile

The Nile, cradling humanity's beginnings, provides many experiences as it meanders through Egypt. A deluxe cruise between Luxor and Aswan is one of the most wonderful ways to discover the Nile. Relax on the terrace as the sun casts its golden colors over the tranquil countryside while enjoying excellent Egyptian and foreign cuisine.

The magnificent Karnak Temple Complex greets you in Luxor. Immerse yourself in the splendor of The Great Hypostyle Hall, an architectural marvel that will take your breath away. The Luxor Temple, a UNESCO World Heritage site, provides a mystical experience as it glows softly at night. Do not pass up the chance to see the Valley of the Kings, a magnificent cemetery that holds the tombs of great pharaohs such as Tutankhamun and Ramses II.

Aswan, Egypt's entrance to Nubia, stands apart from the rest of the country. Its relaxed ambiance and the spectacular scenery of the Nile make it the ideal place to unwind. Visit the breathtaking Abu Simbel Temples carved right into the rock and the Philae Temple, who sings thanks to the goddess Isis. Please stop by the Nubian villages, recognizable by their brightly colored dwellings, and chat with the friendly residents.

Accepting The Future While Honoring The Past

Cairo and the Nile in 2023 are ideally placed at the crossroads of their great history and promising future. Visit the newly opened Grand Egyptian Museum, which displays a massive collection of ancient Egyptian antiquities, including Tutankhamun's stunning burial riches. As the sun sets over the Nile, immerse yourself in Cairo's lively nightlife, with live music and traditional dance performances.

The voyage to Cairo and the Nile is remarkable and will leave you with life-changing experiences and memories. Explore Egypt's history, marvel at its stunning beauty, and love its timeless culture. The year to go on the ultimate Egyptian trip is 2023.

10 INTERESTING REASONS TO VISIT CAIRO AND THE NILE

C onsider Cairo and the Nile as a location for your next journey, with good cause. This travel guide will dig into ten intriguing reasons why you should visit Cairo and the Nile, considering the region's rich history, one-of-a-kind experiences, and stunning scenery.

1. A Step Back in Time: Visiting Cairo and the Nile is like stepping back. Egypt is a treasure mine for history buffs, with an ancient culture extending back thousands of years. There is a seemingly limitless variety of discoveries, from the majestic temples and tombs, including the renowned Pyramids and Sphinx of Giza, to the rich historical treasures at the Egyptian Museum.

2. Vibrant City Life: Cairo is Egypt's bustling metropolis and provides a wide range of cultural activities waiting to be discovered. From colorful marketplaces like the Khan el-Khalili Bazaar to busy streets teeming with people and visitors alike, the city offers an unforgettable experience. Foodies will appreciate trying classic Egyptian street foods like kosher and falafel, while shoppers will enjoy bargaining for the best discounts on souvenirs.

3. Nile River Cruise: A Nile River cruise is a must-do on any vacation to Egypt. This renowned river was an important passage for ancient Egyptians and is still a source of livelihood and transit for the inhabitants. You will be treated to stunning vistas of rural Egypt and its plentiful wildlife as you cruise up the Nile, pausing to visit ancient sites such as the temples of Karnak and Luxor.

4. Egyptian friendliness: The inhabitants are noted for their genuine warmth and friendliness, making your vacation even more memorable. Egyptians eagerly share their rich culture and history with guests, offering anything from guided tours to home-cooked dinners. Engaging with the local community is a great way to learn more about Egyptian customs and everyday life.

5. Diving under the red sea: Consider diving under the surface of the Red Sea if you appreciate aquatic activities. The Red Sea, near Cairo, has interesting marine life and spectacular underwater vistas. This location draws novice and professional divers due to its pure water and beautiful coral reefs. You could even glimpse a whale shark or dolphin during your dive!

6. Islamic cairo: Islamic Cairo is a region famous for its great architectural masterpieces, such as the Al-Azhar Mosque, the Citadel of Saladin, and the Sultan Hassan Mosque. Walking through the small alleyways lined with old houses, a UNESCO World Heritage Site since 1979, will leave you stunned by the fine details and craftsmanship spanning generations.

7. Egyptian Nightlife: Cairo comes alive after the sun goes down. Immerse yourself in a dynamic environment packed with music, dancing, and performances, with various alternatives to satisfy all tastes. Traditional belly dance exhibitions, traditional performances, and contemporary clubs and nightclubs cater to a wide range of preferences. The Cairo Opera House also stages several notable local and international performances throughout the year.

8. Egyptian Street Art: Street art has developed in Cairo recently, presenting a distinct and modern take on the city's culture. Vibrant paintings depict Egyptian history, identity, and culture while commenting on contemporary social and political challenges. Exploring Cairo's burgeoning street art culture is a fantastic opportunity to interact with the city's creativity.

9. Birdwatching Along the Nile: The Nile draws numerous bird species that depend on the river for their habitat as it passes through Egypt. If you like bird watching, look for Egrets, Kingfishers, Black kites, and Grey herons, among others. The tranquil atmosphere will make your stay unforgettable and one-of-a-kind.

10. Embracing Egyptian Creativity: Egypt has a vibrant art scene provides an intriguing view into its culture and present society. Visit galleries and studios across Cairo to immerse yourself in diverse creative forms and expressions, including works by artists who use ancient methods and those that address contemporary subjects and trends.

Starting your Egyptian vacation in Cairo and the Nile will give you a tapestry of history, culture, and natural beauty that few other places can rival. Once you begin on this wonderful adventure, it is simple to see why Egypt has captivated and interested tourists for ages.

15 THINGS TO KNOW BEFORE TRAVELING TO CAIRO AND THE NILE

A s you plan your next trip to this gorgeous place, it is important to be well informed on the distinctive elements of Cairo and the Nile. Here are 15 must-know facts to help you prepare for your Egyptian journey.

1. Documentation and visas: Most visitors to Egypt need a visa, which may be acquired upon arrival. However, before traveling, verify the regulations for your unique nationality. Check that your passport is valid for at least six months from your arrival date.

2. Currency and payments: The Egyptian Pound (EGP) is the local currency. Many hotels, restaurants, and stores take credit cards, but having cash is vital for visiting local markets and paying for transportation or gratuities.

3. Language: The official language is Arabic. However, English is commonly spoken in most tourist locations. Learn basic Arabic phrases to demonstrate your interest in and respect for the local language.

4. Best time to visit: Cairo and the Nile are open yearly. The weather is normally pleasant and agreeable from October through April, with chilly nights. Summer temperatures may rise, so schedule your touring for early mornings and late afternoons to escape the heat.

5. Dress modestly: Egypt is largely an Islamic nation. Thus, conservative attire is preferred. Both men and women are expected to cover their shoulders and knees. When visiting religious locations, bring a headscarf.

6. Security: Cairo and the Nile are generally secure for visitors. However, it is critical to use care in congested locations, avoid wandering alone at night, and watch local news for developments.

7. Transportation: While taxi applications like Uber and Careem are popular for getting about, a guided tour or hiring a private driver will help you navigate, learn, and enjoy the city and its historical beauties better.

8. Pyramid of Giza: The Pyramids of Giza, the Egyptian Museum, and Nile River cruises are among the must-see sights in Cairo. Allow enough time to enjoy these beauties and, if necessary, book reservations in advance.

9. Exploring historical places: Dress comfortably for lengthy days touring historical sites, pack lots of drinks, and protect your skin from the heat with sunscreen, a hat, and sunglasses.

10. Respect Egyptian culture: Before leaving, learn about the local customs and traditions. Respecting Egyptian culture will result in a more friendly and delightful experience throughout your travels.

11. Tipping: Tipping, or baksheesh, is important to Egyptian society. Even if your payment includes a service fee, tip your guides, drivers, and other service providers.

12. Shopping: When shopping, haggling is popular, especially at marketplaces like the famed Khan el-Khalili bazaar. Accept the local culture, and remember that bargaining is an anticipated part of the shopping experience.

13. Egyptian food: Egyptian food is varied and delectable. Try traditional foods like koshary, ta'ameya, and molokhia to taste the local cuisine. Many restaurants cater to foreign tastes as well.

14. Connection: To remain connected when traveling, get a local SIM card or choose an international roaming service. Many hotels and eateries provide free Wi-Fi.

15. Travel insurance: It is strongly recommended that you get adequate travel insurance before your trip. This offers necessary medical coverage and may also cover losses caused by theft, travel cancellations, or delays.

With this information, you will undoubtedly have a memorable and delightful vacation to Cairo and the Nile. Witness the region's stunning history and immerse yourself in the unique Egyptian culture. The adventure is waiting for you!

WHAT TO DO AND NOT TO DO IN CAIRO AND ALONG THE NILE

C airo, Egypt's dynamic city, has a rich history and unique sites that lure many travelers each year. This busy metropolis on the Nile River provides an outstanding blend of old and contemporary culture. Our travel guide will give you important advice and instructions on what to do and what not to do in Cairo and along the Nile to help you make the most of your trip.

Discovering Cairo: Visit The Historic Attractions

A trip to Cairo would only be completed with seeing the magnificent Giza Pyramids and Sphinx. Visiting these ancient sites is essential as one of Egypt's most recognizable icons. Consider hiring a competent guide to give vital knowledge and support in navigating the often busy places.

Cairo also has many fascinating museums that eloquently display Egypt's rich past. The Egyptian Museum, for example, has a collection of over 120,000 ancient antiquities, while the Coptic Museum focuses on art from Egypt's early Christian period. To get the most out of your museum trips, prepare ahead of time by allotting enough time to thoroughly explore the exhibits.

Local Markets To Stroll And Shop

Shopping in colorful bazaars and marketplaces is one of the greatest ways to immerse yourself in the local culture. The Khan el-Khalili market in Cairo's center is an excellent place to purchase authentic Egyptian souvenirs and handicrafts. However, remember that bargaining is necessary in such marketplaces, so do not be afraid to haggle for the best price.

Enjoy Egyptian Cuisine.

Make it a point to try real Egyptian food while in Cairo. ne must-try foods are ful medames (cooked fava beans), ꜣsher (a blend of rice, pasta, and lentils), and shawarma grilled meat wrapped in pita bread). To sample regional cuisines, visit notable street food sellers or renowned restaurants such as Abou El Sid and Kebdet El Prince.

Nile River Cruising

A trip down the Nile River, in addition to Cairo's numerous attractions, provides an amazing experience that lets you view some of the most important ancient sites. To get the most out of your Nile cruise, book with a reliable provider and choose a comfortable vessel that fits your budget and interests.

Luxor has stunning temples and tombs, and Aswan, which has the amazing Abu Simbel Temple, are two crucial places to explore on your Nile trip. Make sure you hire a professional guide to educate you on the historical importance of these locations.

Avoiding Cairo And The Nile

1. Disregarding local conventions: Be aware of Egyptian customs and traditions to guarantee a pleasant and pleasurable journey. Dress modestly, particularly while visiting holy locations, and abstain from public shows of love.

2. Taking images without permission: It is normal to want to capture your travel, but always obtain permission before shooting individuals or specific sites. This shows respect for the local culture and contributes to a good environment.

3. Using just public transportation: Cairo and its surrounding cities may take a lot of work to manage. Consider getting a private automobile or cab to tour the city and its surroundings at your leisure for your convenience and safety.

4. Ignoring safety advice: While Egypt is typically safe for visitors, keeping aware of possible safety issues and adhering to local rules is crucial. Check for and follow any travel warnings issued by your government to ensure a worry-free journey.

You will have a fascinating and enlightening experience if you follow our tips on what to do and what not to do in Cairo and the Nile.

CAIRO AND THE NILE
VISA REQUIREMENTS

I f you want to visit Cairo's seductive treasures and the magnificence of the Nile River in 2023, you must first confirm that you fulfill the visa requirements. To assist you in navigating the process, we have included complete information on visa requirements and other crucial facts you should be aware of while coming to Egypt.

Types Of Visas And Their Duration

Egypt provides numerous visas kinds for visitors based on the purpose of their visit. Tourists visiting Cairo and the Nile are normally given access with a single or multiple-entry visa. A single-entry visa allows for a 30-day stay. Still, a multiple-entry visa permits visitors to depart and re-enter Egypt numerous times within six months, with each entrance allowing for a 30-day stay.

There Are Various Options For Obtaining An Egyptian Visa:

1. Visa on Arrival: Citizens of some countries, including the United States, the United Kingdom, Australia, Canada, and the European Union, may receive a visa on arrival at Egyptian airports. The charge for a visa on arrival is USD 25.

2. Citizens of qualified countries may apply for an e-

Visa online before going to Egypt. The online application process is simple, and most candidates get their approved e-Visa within five business days. The costs for an e-Visa are USD 25 for a single entrance and USD 60 for repeated entries.

3. Egyptian Consulates and Embassies: Travelers from countries not eligible for visas on arrival or e-Visa must apply for a visa at their home country's Egyptian consulate or embassy. Because processing times and expenses vary, verifying with the closest embassy before applying is best.

Eligibility And Documentation

Determining if your nationality necessitates a pre-approved visa, visa on arrival, or e-Visa is essential. While visa requirements vary by place of origin, some common supporting papers include the following:

- A valid passport with at least six months remaining validity from the intended date of entrance
- A visa application form filled out completely and accurately.
- Passport-sized pictures taken recently
- Evidence of adequate finances to pay travel costs
- A confirmed itinerary, including round-trip airfare and hotel accommodations.

Exemptions From Visa

Travelers from a few countries, including Bahrain, Kuwait, Lebanon, Oman, Saudi Arabia, and the United Arab Emirates, are not required to get a visa to enter Egypt for a maximum stay of 90 days.

Furthermore, travelers crossing Egypt for less than 48

hours do not need a visa if they have a confirmed onward ticket. If given clearance by immigration officials, they may tour Cairo and the Nile during their transit stay.

Nile Cruises And Guided Tours

When planning a guided trip or a Nile cruise, check the visa requirements for each stop on the itinerary. While most guided tours take care of such formalities, it is a good idea to double-check if your visa includes all Nile stopovers.

While arranging a vacation to Cairo and the Nile, examining visa requirements and ensuring that all relevant papers are in order is essential. Taking care of these details will help you to have a stress-free journey while immersing yourself in the ancient land's rich history and breathtaking beauty.

IS A VISA REQUIRED TO VISIT CAIRO AND THE NILE?

U nderstanding the visa requirements is an important component of your travel preparations as you plan your trip to the country of pharaohs, pyramids, and the legendary Nile River. This travel guide will teach you about the numerous visa alternatives, requirements, and procedures in order to make your trip to Cairo and the Nile as smooth as possible.

First and foremost, as with any trip arrangements, you must confirm that your passport is valid for at least six months from the day you want to visit Egypt. When you are clear, it is time to think about visa possibilities.

Visa-Free Countries: You are lucky to be a citizen of Bahrain, Hong Kong, Kuwait, Lebanon, Macau, Oman, Saudi Arabia, or the United Arab Emirates! No visa is necessary for less than 90 days in Egypt. This exemption, however, does not apply to Lebanese nationals going for tourist reasons, and a pre-arranged visa is necessary.

Visa on Arrival: Visitors from the United States, the United Kingdom, Canada, Australia, and other European countries may receive a visa on arrival in Egypt. This single-entry visa is valid for up to 30 days. It costs $25, payable in cash or by card at visa-on-arrival counters at Cairo International

Airport and other international airports.

E-Visa: In 2017, the Egyptian government implemented an e-visa system to streamline the procedure for qualifying nations. The e-visa, like the visa on arrival, is normally valid for a 30-day single-entry visit. You may apply for an e-visa online using the official webpage, and you can pay the application cost with a credit or debit card. It is highly advised to apply for your e-visa at least seven days before your travel since processing might take up to seven days.

Pre-Arranged Visa: If you are not qualified for visa exemptions, visa on arrival, or an e-visa, you must apply for a pre-arranged visa at the closest Egyptian consulate or embassy before traveling. Requirements and application processes may differ by country, so check with the Egyptian consulate in your local country for the most current and accurate information.

Numerous-Entry Visas: If your journey to Egypt involves numerous entries, you must apply for a multiple-entry visa. This visa is unavailable on arrival and must be requested through an Egyptian consulate or embassy in your home country. Apply as soon as possible since processing timeframes might vary.

LIST OF COUNTRIES WHOSE RESIDENTS ARE EXEMPT FROM REQUIRING A VISA

A s you plan your trip to this wonderful area of Egypt, you will be relieved to learn that certain nations may visit without a visa. Before we dig into Cairo's awe-inspiring history, culture, and scenic splendor, let us discuss who may avoid the visa-required procedure for their epic voyage.

Citizens Of The Following Countries Are Permitted To Visit Egypt Without Acquiring A Visa In Advance:

- Bahrain, Hong Kong, Kuwait, Lebanon (only for mandatory travel), Macau, Oman, Saudi Arabia, and the United Arab Emirates may visit Egypt for up to 90 days without a visa.

- Travelers with Malaysian or Maldivian passports may stay in Egypt for up to two weeks without a visa.

Meanwhile, nationals of the European Union, the United States, Australia, Canada, New Zealand, South Korea, North Macedonia, and Ukraine, among others, may apply online for a visa on arrival or an electronic visa (e-Visa). However, remember that visa exemption and pre-approved visa issuance are subject to change based on your nationality, the purpose of your visit, and the duration of your stay.

Taking advantage of visa-free travel to Cairo and the Nile. Make the most of your trip by immersing yourself in the region's rich culture and legacy. Discover the magnificent Giza Pyramids and the Great Sphinx, representing the ancient civilization that once thrived around the glorious Nile. Stroll around Islamic Cairo's busy streets, marveling at the breathtaking architecture of mosques and monuments. See the beautiful riches and artifacts in Egypt's most renowned archaeological sites at the legendary Egyptian Museum.

Beyond the city boundaries, a trip to the Nile's banks will open you to a new world of discovery. Board a magnificent Nile cruise ship and travel along the tranquil waterways, admiring the enthralling scenery. As you go down the river, uncover the ancient mysteries of Kom Ombo, Edfu, and Karnak. Do not miss the royal tombs in the famed Valley of the Kings, where ancient Egypt's pharaohs were put to rest.

Travelers may easily see the marvels of Cairo and the Nile amid the seductive aroma of history and the rich tapestry of culture since a significant portion of the world's population enjoys visa-free travel to Egypt.

Remember to check for any modifications to visa restrictions or travel alerts when planning your Egyptian journey since rules and exceptions might change over time. For the most up-to-date information, contact your country's embassy or consulate. This will guarantee a stress-free and wonderful trip to Cairo and the Nile.

Nationals Of The Following Countries Are Exempt From Visa Requirements.

With its renowned Pyramids, busy marketplaces, and huge desert vistas, Egypt awaits your discovery. If you are a citizen of one of the nations mentioned below, you are exempt from visa formalities, making your trip to Egypt easier and less stressful than ever before.

First and foremost, people from many Arab and African countries are excused from acquiring a visa to visit Egypt, making it much simpler to enjoy Cairo's rich history and captivating culture. Citizens of Bahrain, Djibouti, Guinea, Jordan, Kuwait, Lebanon (only if arriving for tourism and possessing a residence permit issued by Saudi Arabia, Kuwait, the United Arab Emirates, or Oman), Libya, Mauritania, Morocco, Oman, Qatar, Saudi Arabia, Somalia, Sudan, Tunisia, the United Arab Emirates, and Yemen are among those eligible.

Furthermore, Egypt and nations in other areas have many arrangements and agreements that exclude their residents from visa requirements. For example, if you are a Malaysian or Bruneian citizen, you will be relieved to hear that you may visit Cairo and the Nile without obtaining a visa.

Furthermore, Chinese individuals who visit Egypt as part of a group trip organized by a licensed Egyptian or Chinese travel operator are free from visa requirements. This agreement enables Chinese visitors to enjoy the wonders of Cairo and the Nile without the burden of acquiring a visa.

Travelers from other countries should check the most current visa laws before organizing a trip to Cairo and the Nile since visa requirements might change. Please remember that to be eligible for these visa exemptions, your passport must be valid for at least six months from your arrival in Egypt.

You can tour historical landmarks such as the Great Pyramids of Giza, the Sphinx, the Egyptian Museum, and the Khan el-Khalili market while in Cairo and the Nile. A Nile cruise will also enable you to see historic temples, tombs, and towns along the river's banks. These sites, and many more, are available without a visa in Cairo and the Nile.

You may plan your vacation without any needless complications now that you know which nations are excluded from visa requirements for Cairo and the Nile. Our travel guide strives to make your trip unforgettable by giving thorough and up-to-date information on all aspects, allowing you to enjoy the greatest historical sites, local food, lodgings, and cultural experiences Egypt offers. Enjoy your journey to Cairo and the Nile!

LIST OF COUNTRIES REQUIRING A VISA TO VISIT CAIRO AND THE NILE

C airo and the Nile: a place rich in history, culture, and stunning scenery that draws visitors worldwide. It is important to know Egypt's current visa requirements when planning your trip to this lovely country. We want to detail the visa procedure for inhabitants of many nations humanely in our thorough 2023 travel guide. Let us get into the specifics and ease your preparation process.

Overview Of Visa Requirements:

Visitors visiting Cairo and the Nile in Egypt must get a visa before commencing their journey. However, the details of the criteria are determined by the traveler's nationality. Some nations have bilateral agreements that free them from obtaining a visa for admission for a specific period. Still, others may need to apply for a visa upon arrival or via an Egyptian consulate before their trip.

Pre-Arrival Visa Requirement Countries:

Citizens of the following countries must get a visa from an Egyptian consulate or embassy in their home country before traveling to Cairo and the Nile region:

- Afghanistan
- Algeria
- Angola
- Azerbaijan
- The Republic of Azerbaijan
- Bangladesh
- Bosnia
- Cameroon
- Iran
- Iraq
- Kazakhstan
- Kazakhstan
- Lebanese
- Liberia
- Mali
- Mauritius
- Republic of Moldova
- Montenegro
- Morocco
- Nepal
- Nigeria
- Pakistan
- The Philippines
- Sierra Leone
- Somaliland
- Sri Lankan
- Sudan
- Syria
- Tunisia
- Vietnam

A pre-arrival visa is required for citizens of these countries, and they must have their visa paperwork with them before entering Egypt.

Visa On Arrival Eligible Countries:

Visitors from the following countries may receive a visa on arrival in Egypt at any major international airport:

- The country of Australia
- Canada
- Japan
- The country of New Zealand
- The United States

Travelers from these countries may acquire a visa at a designated desk upon arrival at Cairo International Airport or any other major airport. Travelers must have a valid passport with at least six months of validity, proof of a confirmed return or onward ticket, and sufficient finances to cover their stay.

E-Visa Eligible Countries:

Egypt has also implemented an electronic visa (e-visa) system for citizens of several countries to streamline the procedure. Visitors from 46 countries, including the visa-on-arrival mentioned earlier and other European and Asian countries, may apply for an e-visa via the official government website.

Citizens of these countries must complete the application with appropriate personal information, passport information, and a valid email address for correspondence reasons. E-visa costs may be paid online, making this a handy and smooth choice for many tourists.

Visa Exemptions And Special Circumstances:

Egypt allows tourists from various countries, mostly the Gulf Cooperation Council (GCC) and North African nations, to enter without a visa for up to 90 days. Bahrain, Kuwait, Oman, Saudi Arabia, the United Arab Emirates, Jordan, Libya, and Yemen are among them.

Furthermore, tourists stopping in Cairo as part of a cruise or with certain kinds of aircraft tickets, such as a direct transit ticket, may not need a visa if their transit period to Egypt is shorter than 48 hours. Check these exclusions and their precise requirements depending on your trip intentions.

Determine and get your visa needs depending on your nationality as a visitor ready to see Cairo and the Nile in 2023. This guide is intended to offer an overview of the different visa kinds and eligibility information. However, before confirming your trip arrangements, we suggest checking Egypt's official consulate or embassy websites to confirm the particular requirements for your nationality since rules may change.

With your visa in hand, it is time to begin your wonderful adventure to Cairo and the Nile, where old civilization's secrets and the grandeur of the world's longest river await you. Best wishes!

AIRPORT TRANSIT VISA

T his detailed book will assist you in navigating the visa procedure and making the most of your trip to the enthralling country of pharaohs, pyramids, and the powerful Nile.

Visa Requirements For Airport Transit

Some passengers may need an airport transit visa while passing through an airport in Egypt, notably in Cairo, the city that never sleeps. An airport transit visa allows temporary entrance into the nation for a limited length of time, often up to 48 hours, but does not allow you to leave the airport. Before going on your adventure, you must establish if you need one.

Travelers from the United States, the European Union, and most other Western countries, as well as numerous African and Asian countries, do not need an airport transit visa as long as they stay inside the airport's international transit area and have onward tickets to their ultimate destinations. On the other hand, citizens of Afghanistan, Bangladesh, Congo, Eritrea, Ethiopia, Iran, Iraq, Lebanon, Palestine, Somalia, and Sri Lanka must get an airport transit visa before visiting Egypt.

How To Obtain An Airport Transit Visa

You should contact the closest Egyptian embassy or consulate in your home country at least several weeks before your travel to apply for an airport transit visa. A completed and signed visa application form, a valid passport with at least six months of validity left, two passport-sized pictures, and a fee payment are normally required. Additional paperwork, such as onward travel tickets or evidence of financial resources, may be requested.

You may also apply online using the Egyptian government's e-Visa system, which enables qualified candidates to apply for and receive an airport transit visa electronically. Establish an account, provide the relevant information, upload the appropriate documents, pay the price, and wait for confirmation. An approved e-Visa will be sent to you, which you should print and bring on your trip.

Consequences Of Duration, Extension, And Overstay

An airport transit visa normally allows for a maximum stay of 48 hours at Cairo Airport's international transit zone or any other Egyptian airport. Extensions are seldom granted; if your transit time is within the allowed stay, you must apply for a standard tourist visa.

Overstaying your transit visa may result in penalties, incarceration, or deportation, as well as issues with future Egyptian travel. To prevent complications during your trip, you must obey the guidelines and respect the term of your visa.

With the proper planning and information, navigating the visa procedures for airport transit in Cairo and the Nile may be straightforward and stress-free. Ensure you have all of the appropriate documentation and protocols before your flight, and enjoy your stopover in Cairo or any other Egyptian airport.

Whether you are traveling through the land of the pharaohs or want to explore its ancient beauties, this guide will help you have a pleasant and interesting trip.

DOCUMENTS NEEDED

When arranging a trip to Cairo and the Nile, it is essential to understand the paperwork needed to guarantee a smooth and memorable experience. This travel guide strives to give all the required material to assist you in navigating this wonderful city and its surroundings.

Passport:
Your passport is a must-have item for foreign travel. To enter and travel inside Egypt, you must have a valid passport. Your passport must be valid for at least six months from nationwide admission. It is also a good idea to bring photocopies of your passport and keep them separate from your original when traveling. If you lose your passport, these duplicates might help you get a new one faster.

Visa:
Egypt visa requirements differ based on your nationality. Most travelers will need a tourist visa to visit Cairo and the Nile, which may be acquired in advance or upon arrival. Tourist visas with single and multiple entries are available for up to three months. Before your journey, you may apply for an e-visa online; check the official websites for the most up-to-date restrictions and costs.

If you come without a pre-arranged visa, you may get one at Cairo International Airport, Hurghada International Airport, Luxor International Airport, and a few additional entry points. Carry two passport-sized pictures and enough money in US dollars, Euros, or British pounds to pay the visa charge.

Travel Protection:
Although not required, buying travel insurance before visiting Cairo and the Nile is strongly advised. This will cover unanticipated medical procedures, emergencies, or other mishaps that may arise during your vacation. Different plans give varying levels of coverage, so take the time to study and choose a plan that meets your travel requirements.

Vaccination History:
While immunizations are not necessary for admission into Egypt, having your records on hand is a good idea. If you are traveling from a country with a current yellow fever epidemic, proof of yellow fever vaccination may be required. Also, ensure you have all your usual vaccines, including measles, mumps, rubella, diphtheria-tetanus-pertussis, and hepatitis B.

Egyptian Pound:
As a visitor, it is essential to have local cash (Egyptian Pounds) on hand for costs like tipping, which is customary in Egypt. In Cairo and other major cities, credit cards are frequently accepted. However, carrying cash, particularly in smaller quantities, will make purchases with tiny enterprises, street sellers, or at more distant spots along the Nile easier.

Itineraries and travel documents:
Document your vacation arrangements, including airline details, hotel bookings, and planned excursions. In case of a disagreement with a service provider, save hard copies

of your itinerary and associated papers. Electronic backups are also useful for accessing critical information on the fly.

Contact Information in Case of Emergency:
Being prepared is essential! Make a list of emergency contact numbers, such as the local embassy or consulate, emergency services, family or friends, and medical institutions nearby. When you have this knowledge readily accessible, it is simpler to deal with unforeseen scenarios.

Codes of Conduct and Cultural Awareness:
It is strongly advised that you bring a guide about Cairo's and the Nile's history and cultural standards. The locals value courteous guests who respect their culture and values. To ensure seamless interactions throughout your trip, familiarize yourself with fundamental social etiquette and Arabic terminology.

Organizing important paperwork and knowing Cairo and the Nile's cultural expectations can help you have a stress-free, enlightening, and memorable vacation. By being well-prepared, you are taking the initial steps toward a successful and wonderful journey.

THE TIME IT TAKES TO GET A VISA

Planning a vacation to Cairo and the Nile in 2023 is a thrilling adventure, and securing a visa is a necessary step. We have put up full information on the time it takes to secure a visa to assist you in negotiating this stage, so you can concentrate on enjoying your visit to the enthralling land of the pharaohs.

Understanding the sort of visa you want and the conditions for obtaining it is essential to ensure a smooth application process. Most visitors visiting Cairo and the Nile will need a short-stay tourist visa. This permits you to remain in Egypt for up to 30 days and may be single-entry or multiple-entry, depending on your itinerary. Please keep in mind that visa requirements and processing timeframes may differ depending on your nationality.

Applying for a visa ahead of time will save you time and possible headaches once you reach Cairo, and it is typically recommended that you start the procedure at least a month before your intended trip. There are various options for acquiring your visa, each with its processing time and price.

1. Visiting your own country's Egyptian Consulate or Embassy

You must submit your passport, two passport-sized

pictures, a completed visa application form, and the visa cost, which may vary from $25 for a single-entry visa to $60 for a multiple-entry visa, to apply for a visa via an Egyptian Consulate or Embassy. Visa processing periods at the embassy vary but may take up to two weeks.

2. Online e-visa application

You may choose an e-visa for a faster procedure, which has been available since 2017. Applying for an e-visa is easy since it saves you time and allows you to do it from your home. You must still provide the relevant documentation, such as a digital picture, a scanned copy of your passport, and trip itinerary (including hotel bookings). An e-visa costs between $25 and $60, including a $3 administrative fee. The processing period for an e-visa is generally less than a week.

3. Obtaining an Arrival Visa

While coming to Egypt without a visa is not ideal, a visa may be obtained upon arrival at Cairo International Airport. Remember that this option is only accessible to inhabitants of qualified countries, such as the United States, the European Union, and Australia. Visa on-arrival payments for a single entry visa are $25, payable in cash. A visa on arrival normally takes 30 minutes to an hour, so please be prepared for any wait durations.

SEVEN DAYS IN CAIRO AND THE NILE - A COMPREHENSIVE 1-WEEK ITINERARY

This one-week holistic travel itinerary will give you a memorable experience in Cairo and along the Nile. With its rich history, culture, and gastronomic pleasures, Cairo will surely leave you with memories that last a lifetime. A trip down the Nile will transport you to ancient Egypt, making your adventure one-of-a-kind and memorable.

Day One: Arrival In Cairo

When you arrive at Cairo International Airport, a quick journey to your hotel will allow you to unpack and recharge for the adventure ahead. Begin your first day with a stroll around Cairo's busy streets. Visit the scenic Garden City neighborhood, which offers a sight of Cairo's rich green spaces, and take advantage of the iconic Tahrir Square, which serves as the heart of contemporary Egypt.

Explore the vibrant world of Egyptian art at the Cairo Opera House in the afternoon, followed by a delicious supper at a classic Egyptian cafe. Finish the evening by strolling through Zamalek's picturesque and vibrant alleyways, an island district in the Nile.

Day 2: Explore Ancient Egypt

A vacation to Cairo would only be complete with seeing the renowned Great Pyramids of Giza and the enigmatic Sphinx. A guided tour will give insight into the interesting history of these age-old global marvels. Following that, dine with a stunning panoramic view of the pyramids.

In the afternoon, visit the Egyptian Museum in downtown Cairo, where you may examine priceless treasures such as Tutankhamun's legendary treasure hoard. As the sun sets, turn your evening into a cultural experience by watching a mesmerizing light and sound extravaganza on the Giza plateau.

Day 3: Islamic Cairo And Old Cairo

Begin your day in Cairo's Coptic neighborhood, where the city's Christian legacy thrives. Before roaming about Khan El-Khalili's lovely market, see the Hanging Church, the Church of St. George, and the Coptic Museum.

Later in the day, visit the Saladin Citadel, a spectacular medieval fortification with a view over Cairo. Close by is the Alabaster Mosque of Muhammad Ali, one of Islamic Cairo's crown jewels. Finish your day by enjoying wonderful street cuisine and shopping for unique Egyptian items in the lively area of El-Hussein.

Day 4: Sailing On The Nile

Bid goodbye to Cairo and set sail on a sumptuous Nile cruise to the ancient towns of Luxor and Aswan. Your first destination will be the magnificent Temples of Karnak and Luxor, which are well-illuminated and worth seeing at dusk.

Spend the evening enjoying onboard entertainment and interacting with other passengers, all while savoring the exquisite foods available via the cruise's dining selections.

Day 5: Valley Of The Kings And Other Highlights

The renowned Valley of the Kings, a massive cemetery holding the tombs of Egypt's greatest pharaohs, is the next stop on your tour. You may marvel at Tutankhamun's colorful and well-maintained tomb here.

Explore the spectacular Temple of Queen Hatshepsut and the enormous Colossi of Memnon in the afternoon. As night sets, you may rest and refresh aboard your Nile cruise, preparing for the next day's excursions.

Day 6: Aswan Dam And Ancient Temples

Visit the magnificent Temple of Kom Ombo, dedicated to the gods Sobek and Haroeris, as your cruise approaches Aswan. Then, continue south to see the Temple of Edfu, which has well-preserved sculptures and images of Egyptian mythology.

Tour the spectacular Aswan High Dam in the late afternoon, a contemporary engineering wonder that plays an important role in regional water management. Enjoy the vistas before returning to your sailboat for one more Nile leisure and celebration night.

Day 7: Return To Cairo Via Abu Simbel

Finish your vacation with an optional visit to the stunning Abu Simbel temples. These magnificent structures, carved from solid rock cliffs, demonstrate the skill and brilliance of ancient Egyptian construction and design.

Return to Aswan for a relaxed day by the Nile before boarding a flight back to Cairo. One more evening in this pulsing metropolis will allow you to have a goodbye supper while reflecting on your amazing trip.

You will leave Cairo and the Nile with a treasure trove of memories, vivid visuals, and an increased understanding of Egypt's rich past. Your week-long trip to Cairo and the Nile will certainly be a once-in-a-lifetime event you will remember for the rest of your life if you follow this complete itinerary.

HOW TO GET AROUND CAIRO AND THE NILE

E xploring the beauties of Cairo and the Nile can be a riveting experience, and learning how to traverse the area properly is the key to a successful and pleasurable trip. With so many transportation alternatives accessible, getting acquainted with the most efficient and convenient mode of transit is generally beneficial.

Getting Around Cairo's Busy Streets

Cairo, Egypt's enormous metropolis, may be overwhelming for first-time visitors. Because the city is notorious for its severe traffic and congested streets, patience is required while attempting to travel. You may, however, comfortably explore the city's rich history and culture if you grasp the various transit alternatives.

The Cairo Metro: A Quick And Affordable Alternative

Many individuals choose the Cairo Metro because it is both inexpensive and efficient. The metro, which has three lines that span a considerable area of the city, is often the fastest method to go from one location to another while avoiding the clogged highways above. Stations are typically well-kept and safe, making this an excellent choice for passengers seeking convenience and cost-effectiveness.

Taxis: A Convenient But Expensive Option

Taxis are available throughout Cairo and provide a more customized kind of transportation. While cabs are often more expensive than choices, they are still inexpensive by Western standards. Drivers do not use meters, so carefully haggle the cost before leaving. In Cairo, ride-hailing applications like Uber and Careem are accessible, making obtaining a cab even more simple and secure.

Embrace Cairo's Local Charm With Microbuses

Microbuses are a common mode of transportation in Cairo, albeit they may be alarming to foreigners. These privately owned minivans run on defined routes and are a highly cost-effective mode of transportation. Microbuses will offer you a genuine experience of Cairo's local character after you get acquainted with the routes and the procedure of boarding and disembarking.

Cruising Down The Nile

The Nile River has long been Egypt's lifeline, and journey to the country would only be complete with seeing its intriguing waters. A Nile cruise is a one-of-a-kind and fascinating opportunity to see this lovely river and its surroundings.

Nile Cruises: Explore Egypt's Ancient Wonders In Luxury

A Nile cruise is an excellent way to see Upper Egypt's numerous treasures, offering a pleasant and comfortable ride through the river's stunning and ancient scenery.

These cruises typically span three to seven days and include visits to famous ancient sites, including Luxor, Aswan, Abu Simbel, and Kom Ombo.

A Traditional Sailing Adventure In Feluccas

Consider a felucca ride for a more personal and genuine Nile experience. Feluccas are classic wooden sailboats that have been a part of Egypt's nautical heritage for generations; these boats enable you to enjoy the tranquil beauty of the Nile at your leisure. Feluccas may be found in Cairo, Luxor, and Aswan, with cruises ranging from a few hours to overnight adventures.

Traveling By Train Between Cairo, Luxor, And Aswan

Trains provide an effective and picturesque mode of transportation between Cairo, Luxor, and Aswan. Egyptian Railways connects these towns regularly, providing a handy way to tour the capital and the Nile River valley. While rail travel is typically pleasant, tickets should be purchased well in advance, especially for overnight sleeper trains.

To summarize, several transportation choices exist for touring Cairo and the Nile. By being acquainted with the numerous kinds of transportation accessible and organizing your trip appropriately, you can maximize your Egyptian vacation by immersing yourself in this wonderful area's remarkable sights, sounds, and sensations.

A GUIDE TO PUBLIC TRANSIT

Discovering Cairo and the Nile area is a memorable experience in and of itself, and navigating its lively streets and rivers using public transit can be an adventure in and of itself. This chapter will give an in-depth overview of the different types of public transportation, ensuring you can go from point A to point B quickly while immersing yourself in the rich tapestry of Egyptian life.

Metro

The Cairo Metro is a fast, cheap, and pleasant form of transit. It is the first in Africa and the Arab world, operating since 1987. It has three lines that cross the city and span a total distance of 100.9 kilometers, serving millions of people every day.

Line 1 (the red line) runs north from El Marg to the south from Helwan. Line 2 (the yellow line) runs from El Monib in the south to Shubra in the north, passing through downtown Cairo and the Giza plateau. Line 3 (the green line) now runs from Attaba to Adly Mansour on a shorter route, intending to expand it further.

Metro tickets are charged based on distance, with one-way rides beginning at 5 EGP. Tickets may be bought at each station's ticket booth.

Microbuses And Buses

Cairo's bus system is a vast network that works from early morning till late at night. Several bus kinds range in size, comfort, and destination. Standard public buses are the least expensive alternative. However, they might be congested during peak hours. Air-conditioned buses are more expensive, but they provide greater comfort.

Microbuses, in addition to ordinary buses, are a popular mode of transportation among residents. These are privately run 14-seater minibusses that go on specific routes that are typically comparable to normal buses. They, like taxis, maybe waved down and only need payment upon disembarking.

You may utilize public transportation applications like SWVL and Buseet to identify the best bus route for your location, including projected trip times, ticket costs, and live bus monitoring.

Apps For Taxis And Ridesharing

Taxis are a more convenient and customized way to see Cairo and the Nile Valley. Traditional black-and-white taxis are metered. However, it is best to negotiate the cost with the driver before beginning your trip. Yellow and white taxi taxis may also be reserved by phone or Internet services.

Ride-hailing applications have also grown in popularity in Cairo, with Uber and Careem being the most popular. These applications provide a convenient, low-cost, and user-friendly alternative to regular taxis.

Nile Taxis And Ferries

The Nile River is an important aspect of Egypt's transportation infrastructure, with several ferries regularly running between its eastern and western banks. These dependable boats are excellent for traveling between Nile-side towns while avoiding gridlock.

For a more customized experience, employ the Nile Taxi service, which runs a fleet of on-demand water taxis. This service is ideal for guests wishing to explore Cairo or its neighboring areas in elegance, with set costs and handy pick-up spots.

Cairo and the Nile area provide various public transportation alternatives to meet the demands of any tourist. The city's metro, bus, and taxi systems give an efficient, economical, and accessible way to experience the city's rich metropolitan environment. In contrast, the legendary Nile waterways provide a once-in-a-lifetime chance for a picturesque and quiet ride into Egypt's heart.

THE BEST WAYS TO GET AROUND CAIRO AND THE NILE

C airo, Egypt's busy and ancient city along the Nile River, has a plethora of transportation alternatives for those wishing to see its sights and cultural treasures. This chapter focuses on assisting you in easily and pleasantly navigating the city and its surroundings.

Exploring Cairo and the Nile necessitates navigating various terrains and traffic scenarios. While Cairo is infamous for its chaotic streets and traffic congestion, using local public transit may be an inexpensive and sometimes faster method to get about. At the same time, there are more comfortable choices for individuals who want a more quiet and calm encounter.

Cairo's Public Transportation

1. The Metro System

The Cairo Metro is one of the city's most efficient transportation modes. It comprises three lines span many of the Greater Cairo region, including stations at notable attractions such as Ramses Station, Tahrir Square, and the Giza Pyramids. Trains run every 5 to 10 minutes during peak hours and every 10 to 15 minutes during off-peak hours. Fares are low, ranging from EGP 5 to EGP 10, depending on the number of stops.

2. Buses

In Cairo, buses are a popular mode of public transit. They might be extremely congested during peak hours, but they provide a genuine local experience. Prices are modest, with most trips costing just a few Egyptian pounds. Bus lines link many city regions; acquaint yourself with their itineraries beforehand or ask locals for guidance.

3. Microbuses

Microbuses are another inexpensive and popular mode of transportation in the city. They are privately owned and operate on a fill-and-go basis, with no regular timetables. Hail a microbus from the side of the road and tell the driver your destination. The fare will be arranged beforehand, so be prepared to fight for a fair deal. Remember that microbuses are less comfortable than other modes of public transit.

Private Transportation Alternatives

1. Taxis

Taxis are commonly accessible in Cairo and provide a handy method to travel about, particularly for individuals who want a private ride. Cabs are classified into classic white and black cabs, yellow-metered taxis, and white-metered taxis. White-metered taxis are government-regulated and have higher requirements, such as air conditioning, making them a more pleasant alternative.

2. Apps for Ride-Hailing

In Cairo, ride-hailing applications such as Uber and Careem

are an alternative to regular taxis. These applications improve price transparency and enable you to monitor your progress. They are also useful for traveling in locations with limited public transportation choices or at night, when public transportation may need to be more dependable.

3. Vehicle Rental

Those who want to explore Cairo and its surroundings at their leisure can consider renting a vehicle. However, owing to the severely crowded traffic and occasionally irregular driving behaviors of native motorists, vigilance is required while driving in Cairo. Furthermore, parking might be difficult, particularly in congested neighborhoods. Hiring a vehicle with a driver who is acquainted with the local roads and traffic laws is strongly advised.

Exploring The Nile Valley

1. Cruises on the Nile

Nile cruises provide a magnificent and pleasant opportunity to see some of Egypt's most renowned sights. The classic route connects Luxor with Aswan via the Temple of Karnak, the Valley of the Kings, and the Abu Simbel Temples. Cruises last three to seven days and vary in luxury and facilities aboard.

2. Trains

The Egyptian National Railways (ENR) links numerous towns along the Nile, providing visitors with an alternate method to explore the riverbanks. There are many railway classes, including air-conditioned first and second classes, and a premium sleeper train between Cairo and Aswan. Booking a train journey is an inexpensive and effective method to travel between major Nile attractions.

Create a genuinely immersive and unforgettable experience in this culturally rich area by learning the numerous alternatives for traveling about Cairo and the Nile. Choosing appropriate forms of transportation depending on your tastes, budget, and travel objectives helps to a hassle-free and delightful tour across Egypt's capital and its captivating Nile scenery.

HOW TO USE THE CAIRO METRO AND THE NILE

The Cairo Metro is not only a vital form of transit for the busy city and its satellite communities but also serves as a gateway to the ancient and contemporary attractions along the Nile. With over 65 stations and three lines covering 80 kilometers, the metro system offers an affordable, dependable, and (at times) less hectic alternative to driving around Cairo. This chapter will teach you all you need to know about utilizing the Cairo Metro to maximize your Egyptian experience in 2023.

Understanding The Stations And Lines

Line 1 (also known as "the Helwan-Marg line" or "the Redline"), Line 2 ("the Shobra El-Kheima - El-Mounib Shobra" or "the Yellow line"), and Line 3 ("the Attaba-El-Abassiya-El-Abbassiyya-Heliopolis-Cairo Airport line" or "the Greenline") are the Cairo Metro's operating lines. Each line is color-coded, making it simple to recognize and distinguish them.

Line 1 connects Helwan and New El-Marg, with stations in Maadi, Sayeda Zeinab, Ramses, and Giza. This route is ideal for exploring locations south of Cairo along the Nile.

Line 2: Line 2 connects Shobra El-Kheima to El-Mounib, including significant stops like Sadat (Tahrir Square), Opera, and Cairo University. This route is a great option for travelers who want to see the Egyptian Museum, the Cairo Opera House, and the world-famous Pyramids of Giza.

Route 3: This route links Cairo's northeastern fringes (Adly Mansour) to the southwestern area, stopping via the important districts of Heliopolis and Nasr City before arriving at Cairo International Airport. It facilitates airport travel while offering access to Coptic Cairo monuments such as the Hanging Church and the Museum of Islamic Art.

How To Ride The Cairo Metro

1. Tickets and fares: At every metro stop, you may buy a single-ride ticket or a multi-use rechargeable card called "The Smart Card." A one-way trip costs 5 and 10 EGP, depending on the number of stations visited.

2. Operating hours: The metro runs from 5:30 a.m. to 12:30 a.m., with trains coming every 5-8 minutes during peak hours and every 10 minutes during off-peak hours. Check the timetable for your specific line and destination.

3. ladies-only coaches: Each train features two cars just for ladies. While women are not required to utilize these carriages, they might be useful for those wanting a less crowded or more pleasant ride, particularly during peak hours.

4. politeness and safety: Being conscious of local traditions and politeness is essential when taking the Cairo metro. Eat, drink, and smoke are prohibited inside railway stops or on the train. Maintaining vigilance over your things and avoiding exhibiting pricey objects that may draw unwanted notice. Finally, to fit in with the locals, observe cultural conventions and dress modestly.

Taking The Metro To See Cairo's Landmarks:

The Metro system in Cairo is fantastic since it makes many renowned places readily accessible, enabling you to see the city without the trouble of bargaining with cabs or managing traffic. Here's how to use the metro to go to some of Cairo's best attractions:

1. Disembark at Sadat station, only a few minutes walk from Tahrir Square and the Egyptian Museum. Prepare to be astounded by ancient Egypt's relics and riches.

2. Giza Pyramids: Take Line 2 to Giza station, then a short taxi or minibus journey to the Giza Plateau.

3. Coptic Cairo: Visit the medieval churches of Coptic Cairo by taking Line 1 to Mar Girgis station and immersing yourself in Egypt's rich heritage of early Christianity.

4. Khan El-Khalili Bazaar: Take Line 1 to Attaba and meander around the bustling marketplaces for a one-of-a-kind shopping experience.

5. Cairo International Airport: Take Line 3 to or from the Cairo Airport station for a hassle-free commute to and from the airport.

The Cairo Metro is a must-have for visitors wishing to discover the city's riches and attractions. By being acquainted with the metro lines, stops, and suggestions for a pleasant journey, you will be ready to explore Cairo and the Nile utilizing this efficient and economical transportation system.

HOW TO OPERATE A TRAM

Traversing Cairo's crowded and ancient city may be a thrilling yet intimidating experience for first-time tourists. Trams, for example, are important in linking people and visitors to the city's wide metropolitan districts. This chapter provides a comprehensive guide on navigating Cairo's tram system easily, comfortably, and confidently.

Recognizing The Tram System

Cairo's large tram network comprises multiple lines systematically planned around the city, connecting significant districts, tourist sites, and transportation hubs. The system, one of the oldest in Africa, has evolved into a crucial artery of Cairo's frenetic everyday life, offering it an efficient and cost-effective means to tour the city and beyond. Tram cars normally run from early morning to midnight, with regular daily service.

The trams are rather simple to recognize since they are painted in brilliant reds and blues and decorated with the phrase "Tramway" or " in Arabic, which can assist you in making your way to the next tram stop.

Getting Your Ticket

To ride the trams, you must first purchase a ticket, which

can be purchased from ticket counters at tram stations in either single or return options. Fares are generally inexpensive, making the trams an affordable option for budget travelers. Remember that as a foreigner, you may be subject to a slightly higher fare than locals, so always carry small currency denominations to make the ticket-buying process go more smoothly.

Using The Tram Routes

Cairo's tram system is well-integrated into the city's transportation networks, so these streetcars frequently service important routes. To navigate the system and plan your route, use a printed tram route map available at stations or consult online resources like interactive city maps, which can provide real-time public transportation updates.

Because tram routes are extensive, take note of your destination and departure stations, which are usually displayed at the stop or printed on your ticket; announcements on the tram may not always be in English, so familiarizing yourself with the route before your journey can be very helpful.

Aboard And Departure

When waiting for your tram, stand patiently behind the designated waiting areas on the platform. Once the tram arrives, allow alighting passengers to exit before boarding. Trams have dual entrance and exit systems, with clearly marked doors for each. Trams can get crowded during peak hours, so always be mindful of your belongings and space.

Keep your ticket handy and follow any instructions given by tram staff while onboard. Stay aware of your surroundings and prepare to descend as your stop approaches. Tram cars usually slow down significantly when approaching stations, giving you ample time to prepare for your exit. Press the stop request button or pull the cord to signal that you wish to alight; however, most stops are mandatory, so there is no need to request a stop in many cases.

Tips And Etiquette

Using Cairo's trams, like any public transportation system, adheres to a set of unwritten conventions that aim to provide everybody a pleasant and orderly experience. To that end, consider the following useful hints:

1. Give up your seat to travelers who are old, crippled, pregnant, or traveling with small children.
2. Keep talks respectable and avoid loud or disruptive conduct.
3. Avoid eating or drinking aboard; always dispose of waste in designated containers.
4. Respect local norms and attempt to dress and behave modestly.
5. Keep an eye on your valuables, particularly during busy hours.

You are now well-equipped to navigate Cairo and the Nile by tram, whether sightseeing or heading to a local eatery; embracing the tram experience allows you to immerse yourself in the rhythm of daily Egyptian life and deepen your travel memories.

THE MOST EFFECTIVE
METHOD OF RIDING
THE BUS

Navigating the bustling city of Cairo and the enchanting Nile region can be an exciting experience, but mastering the local transportation system is critical to making the most of your trip. Using the public bus network is one of the most affordable and convenient ways of getting around, and with a few vital tips and tricks, you, too, can learn the best way to ride the bus in Cairo and the Nile comfortably and enjoyably.

Understanding Cairo's Bus System

Cairo has a large bus network managed by many firms, which may perplex first-time visitors; the key to a successful bus ride is to recognize the range of buses available.

- Public Buses: While the massive, orange buses make up the bulk of Cairo's bus fleet, they may be packed and are not air-conditioned, so be prepared for a hotter experience.
- Microbuses: These white and extensively utilized minibusses are smaller and more casual, stopping at fewer defined areas and following no apparent timetable; they are somewhat more expensive than public buses but normally speedier and occasionally air-conditioned.

- Air-Conditioned Buses: These huge, blue buses, operated by the Cairo Transport Authority (CTA), normally go following established routes and provide a more pleasant journey.

Locating Your Bus Route

Because of the absence of clear maps and schedules, the bus network in Cairo may be difficult to understand. Here are some tips to assist you in discovering the suitable bus and route for your travel needs:

- Local Knowledge: Cairo people are generally kind and can frequently direct you to the proper bus or stop; do not hesitate to ask for help!
- Online Maps: Google Maps has recently begun to include Cairo bus routes, making it a handy resource for planning trips.
- Bus stations: Many Cairo bus stations have listings of routes and destinations; look for them to get an idea of which buses run to your target area.

Pricing And Ticketing

The cost of a bus journey in Cairo and the Nile Valley varies depending on the kind of bus you travel; here's what you need to know:

- Public Buses: You will pay for these buses upon boarding, presenting your money to the driver or fare collector; have smaller change on hand, and anticipate paying between EGP 2 and EGP 3 for a single voyage.
- Microbuses: You normally pay the driver after the voyage, and fares vary based on distance traveled, so expect to pay anywhere from EGP 3 to EGP 15 or more.
- Air-Conditioned Buses: Air-conditioned bus tickets may

be purchased at specialized kiosks or sellers at major bus stops, with prices ranging from EGP 5 to EGP 10, depending on the route.

Tips On Bus Etiquette

Here are some essential tips to make your bus ride more enjoyable:

- Local Customs: Egypt has conservative cultural values. Therefore, it is important to dress modestly and follow seating arrangements. On public buses, ladies traditionally sit in the front, while males sit in the back.
- Maintaining Vigilance: Keep an eye on your possessions since public transit attracts tiny burglars.
- Timing: Cairo traffic is unpredictable, and buses do not stick to a fixed timetable, so plan your trip with enough wiggle space for delays or unexpected diversions.

To summarize, using the bus in Cairo and the Nile area is a genuine way to experience the local transportation system, and with an awareness of the numerous bus choices, route planning, tickets, and local etiquette, your bus travel can be both hassle-free and pleasurable.

HOW TO GO TO
THE AIRPORT

The exciting journey to explore Cairo and the Nile begins and ends with a trip to Cairo International Airport (CAI). In this chapter, we have compiled a detailed guide on how to get to the airport, covering various modes of transportation available, currency exchange tips, and important details to remember while navigating the airport's bustling and ever-changing landscape.

Cairo International Airport, located about 15 miles (24 kilometers) northeast of the city center, is the primary gateway to Egypt, with three main passenger terminals and facilities to cater to the diverse needs of travelers. Given Cairo's thriving tourism scene, it is critical to be well-informed about modes of transportation and the nuances of navigating the city to make your journey as smooth and hassle-free as possible.

Taxis and ride-hailing services:
The most convenient way to get to the airport is to take a taxi or book a rideshare service. Uber and Careem are popular ridesharing apps that can be downloaded on smart devices. With these services, you can fix your fare and avoid haggling or dealing with misinformation on costs. Yellow and white taxis are also easily found throughout the city. Be sure to negotiate a price with the driver before entering a

non-metered cab to avoid overcharging.

Airport Shuttle Service:
The Cairo Airport, Shuttle Bus service, offers an affordable and comfortable way to get to the airport; buses are air-conditioned and have plenty of luggage space, ensuring a stress-free ride. The service operates around the clock, with departure points throughout Cairo and Giza, including Ramses Square, New Cairo, Al Rehab, and Heliopolis. Tickets can be purchased at designated bus stops or online through the Cairo Airport Shuttle Bus website.

Metro and buses are two modes of public transportation.
Cairo's public transportation system is extensive, and while there may be more comfortable options, it is quite affordable. The metro system connects various parts of the city, with the closest station to the airport being El Shams Club Station. Take the metro to El Shams Club Station, then board a minibus or a taxi to the airport.

Private Car Service and Rentals:
Private automobile services may be suitable for individuals who desire individualized attention and comfort when going to Cairo International Airport. Many hotels provide transport services to their guests, so check with your hotel to see if one is available. Alternatively, if you have been using a rental vehicle throughout your stay in Cairo, various car rental businesses provide drop-off services at the airport.

Currency Exchange Suggestions:
Travelers should bring enough local money, Egyptian pounds, to cover transportation and other expenditures. Currency exchange services are accessible at the airport, although, for better rates, it is best to convert money at

banks or official currency exchange offices in the city. Save some little coins for tips or emergencies on your journey to the airport.

Based on your choices, price, and time limits, there are many methods to go to Cairo International Airport. Familiarizing yourself with the different transportation alternatives and having a strategic plan can make your airport trip pleasurable and stress-free. Cairo and the Nile await your discovery, and adopting the essential measures will set the scene for an unforgettable journey in this fascinating part of the globe.

THE GREATEST TIME TO VISIT CAIRO AND THE NILE IS DURING THE SUMMER

In this enthralling chapter, we'll talk about the best time to visit Cairo and the Nile. Egypt, one of the world's most enticing and mysterious places, always captivates travelers with its millennia-old history, renowned monuments, and lively culture. Plan your trip carefully and read about the ideal times to visit this fascinating city to get the most out of Cairo and the Nile.

Egypt is predominantly a desert nation, with weather varying from hot summers to moderate winters. You can anticipate hot, dry, and sunny weather throughout the year. Seasonal and geographical differences, on the other hand, might improve your travel experience, making it critical to determine when to go on your adventure.

From October to April, the "winter" months are often ideal for visiting Cairo and the Nile. It's important to remember, though, that winters in Egypt are nothing like those in the rest of the world. High temperatures seldom fall below 20°C (68°F), although nights may be significantly colder, averaging 10°C (50°F).

During these months, you may easily visit Cairo's ancient

monuments, like the Pyramids of Giza, the Sphinx, and the Egyptian Museum. The dynamic city is a cultural hotspot, with activities such as shopping in the famed Khan el-Khalili market and a magnificent sunset from the Citadel of Saladin.

This time of year on the Nile River is ideal for a cruise between Luxor and Aswan. It has beautiful weather and spectacular festivities, such as the Abu Simbel Sun Festival in February and October. Visitors come to the massive temples during these occasions to see a breathtaking visual spectacle as the sun's rays light the temples' inner sanctums.

May Through September Are The Most Difficult Months.

The Egyptian summer is in full swing from May through September. Cairo and the Nile Valley are scorching hot, often exceeding 40°C (104°F). The oppressive heat may be difficult, particularly when viewing outdoor sights like the Pyramids and the Valley of the Kings.

However, if you can withstand extreme temperatures, there are certain benefits to traveling during the peak summer season. Because it is considered the low season, you may expect fewer people at main sites and better discounts on lodgings and excursions.

Festivals And Ramadan

While planning your vacation, remember the Egyptian calendar and how it may affect your whole experience. Ramadan, which normally falls between April and May, is distinguished by daytime fasting and reduced work hours. Although traveling during Ramadan gives a unique cultural experience, it may make eating and general travel difficult for people unfamiliar with the holy month's rituals.

On the other hand, Egypt's rich festival calendar provides many enjoyable experiences, such as the Cairo International Film Festival in November and the Luxor African Film Festival in March. These enthralling festivals promote the country's culture, heritage, and history, leaving every visitor with a memorable impression.

Managing Crowds And Weather

Cairo and the Nile, like any other tourist site, endure weather and crowd changes. Finding a happy medium between good weather and reasonable crowds is the most dependable strategy. Overall, the months of October, November, February, and March make the Cairo and Nile trip pleasant.

Your objectives and tastes will determine the optimum time to visit Cairo and the Nile. While the milder months of October through April provide pleasant weather, each season has a distinct appeal. Cairo and the Nile are bound to stimulate your senses and increase your grasp of humanity's incredible history, whether you want to brave the heat for fewer people or attend a bustling cultural event.

BEST TIME TO VISIT FOR VARIOUS TRAVELERS

Cairo, the Nile's gem, is a bustling metropolis rich in architectural treasures and historical history. From the towering Pyramids of Giza to the colorful marketplaces of Khan el-Khalili, this African gateway is best visited at the correct time to appreciate the city and its surroundings. The optimum time to see Cairo and the Nile may differ depending on your choices and interests. In this chapter, we will help you identify the best time to visit, whether you are a history buff, an explorer, a budget traveler, or a couple on a romantic break.

For History Buffs, The Months Of October Through April Are Ideal.

If you want to immerse yourself in ancient Egyptian history, the ideal time to visit Cairo and the Nile is during Egypt's autumn and winter months, from October to April. This time of year has the most pleasant weather for touring, with temperatures ranging from 20 to 25°C, making it ideal for seeing the awe-inspiring monuments like the Pyramids, Sphinx, Saqqara, Dahshur, and the vast Egyptian Museum.

During this time, you may also go farther afield to the Nile Valley, where temples, tombs, and ancient treasures await you at Luxor, Aswan, and Abu Simbel. The colder temperatures and bright sky are ideal for investigating these Egyptian artifacts.

September Through May Is The Best Time For Outdoor Enthusiasts And Adventurers.

If you like outdoor activities like camel trekking, hot air ballooning, or scuba diving, the ideal time to visit Cairo and the Nile is from September to May. The good weather conditions during this season provide perfect possibilities to explore the desert, enjoy hot air balloon flights above Luxor's Valley of the Kings, or plunge into the Red Sea's crystal-clear waters.

In addition to these activities, the Nile Valley attracts a variety of migrating bird species throughout the winter months, making it a popular bird-watching destination. You may also visit the White Desert, just a few hours from Cairo, or take a Nile cruise between Luxor and Aswan to enjoy the breathtaking scenery.

May Through September Are The Best Months For Budget Travelers.

During the scorching summer months of May to September, which also coincide with Egypt's low tourism season, Cairo and the Nile attract fewer tourists. If you're on a limited budget and don't mind the heat, now is a perfect time to get amazing prices on flights, accommodations, and guided tours. You'll also be able to see the key sights without the typical crowd.

However, it is crucial to note that temperatures may reach 40°C during these months, particularly in the Nile Valley's southern section. Sightseeing might be difficult, especially between 11 a.m. and 3 p.m. As a result, it is best to plan your trips in the early morning or late afternoon and to remain hydrated.

October Through April Are Ideal Months For Couples For Romantic Getaways.

Cairo and the Nile have an unmistakable allure that draws couples from all over the globe for romantic escapes. Love is undoubtedly in the air, whether seeing the sun setting over the Pyramids, meandering through the labyrinthine lanes of Islamic Cairo, or taking a typical felucca (sailboat) trip on the Nile.

Couples should visit Cairo and the Nile from October to April when the weather is at its finest, and the rich blossoms along the river banks provide an added touch of romanticism. Furthermore, luxury Nile boats provide a wonderful and personal opportunity to tour the magnificent temples and tombs while dining under the stars and enjoying panoramic river views.

Finally, Cairo and the Nile provide many experiences for travelers. Knowing what you want from your vacation and selecting the best time to visit Egypt will ensure an outstanding Egyptian journey. So pack your luggage and prepare to be enchanted by the Nile's charm!

BACKPACKERS' BEST TIME TO VISIT

When is the ideal time for backpackers to visit Cairo and the Nile? With its infinite cultural and historical attractions, any time is a good time to backpack around Egypt. While this is true to some degree, other things to consider, such as weather, seasonal attractions, and economic limits, may impact when visitors choose to visit this magnificent region.

Below, we'll go through the best times to visit Cairo and the Nile to have the most rewarding backpacking experience and make your trip one to remember.

Temperature And Weather

The climate is undoubtedly one of the most important elements to consider while considering a vacation to Egypt. The nation has a desert environment, which implies scorching temperatures, particularly during the summer.

Summer in Egypt is hot and dry, with temperatures in Cairo and other regions often topping 37°C (99°F). This may not be the best time to visit for travelers not acclimated to such high heat since sightseeing may become quite an agony.

In terms of weather, the milder months of October through April are considered the finest time to visit Egypt. Temperatures are often more acceptable during these months, ranging from 15°C to 25°C (59°F to 77°F). The winter months (December to February) are the coldest, making them ideal for seeing historic sites and monuments without sweat.

Tourism And Crowds

Another factor to consider while organizing your backpacking trip to Egypt is the number of visitors that visit the country. The prominent monuments, such as the Great Pyramids, the Valley of the Kings, and the Temples of Luxor and Karnak, may get rather congested during peak tourist season, which runs from October to April. This may detract from the entire experience since managing big crowds of visitors can be difficult for travelers who seek a more immersed and personal encounter.

On the other hand, traveling during the low season (summer) means fewer people and, in many cases, shorter lines at famous attractions. While the heat might be oppressive at this time, travelers who are willing to withstand the heat can explore the major sites without the rush and bustle of a packed tourist spot.

Budget And Costs

The cost of travel may be a major factor in determining the ideal time to visit Cairo and the Nile for budget-conscious backpackers. Prices for lodging, guided excursions, and transportation tend to rise during peak season owing to increased demand. However, these rates often fall during the low season, making it a more affordable alternative for hikers.

Furthermore, during the low season, certain hotels and hostels provide reductions in their prices, offering further opportunities for backpackers to save money and stretch their budget further during their trip.

Festivals And Special Events

Throughout the year, Cairo and the Nile region host many cultural, religious, and musical festivals, some of which might add color and excitement to your backpacking experience. For example, the Cairo International Film Festival attracts filmmakers and film lovers from across the globe every November, while the yearly Nile Festival in February has traditional Egyptian music and dance performances.

By timing your trip to coincide with one or more of these festivals, you will enhance your backpacking experience with cultural activities that give further insight into Egyptian culture and history.

Considering the abovementioned criteria, the ideal period for backpackers to visit Cairo and the Nile is from October to April, when the temperature is milder and more suitable for touring and exploration. On the other hand, the summer months might be a cost-effective option for travelers who want to see the major sights without the crowds and are ready to brave the heat.

Whatever time of year you choose to visit Cairo and the Nile, one thing is certain: the experiences and memories you'll have will be the epitome of a once-in-a-lifetime backpacking journey.

WHEN IS THE BEST TIME TO VISIT FOR A HONEYMOON?

C airo and the Nile Valley give a honeymoon setting that is both engaging and alluring, with seductive history, stunning vistas, and an unequaled combination of old and contemporary cultures. To make the most of your romantic trip to Egypt, choose the best time of year to enjoy the breathtaking scenery, alluring night sky, and tranquil environment this country offers. Allow this chapter to guide you on your adventure to determine the optimum time to visit Cairo and the Nile for an amazing honeymoon experience.

The weather is the most important aspect in deciding when to go on a romantic adventure in Cairo and the Nile. Egypt is recognized for its warm, sunny environment, and the country near the Nile endures minor temperature and humidity changes. Avoiding the desert's heat and the possible discomfort of huge visitor throngs is critical. With this in mind, October to April provide the most moderate weather and a quieter, more intimate setting for your honeymoon.

When the blistering summer heat declines and the gentle autumn light pours down on Cairo and the Nile, the fall season from late October to November is your doorway to the charm of Egypt. This time of year is great for visiting the magnificent Pyramids of Giza and strolling the busy alleys of Cairo's Khan el-Khalili market with your loved one. Furthermore, since the Nile's water levels are at their highest during these months, a romantic river cruise aboard a classic felucca or a deluxe dahabiya will be a once-in-a-lifetime experience. The days are pleasant and comfortable, with temperatures ranging from 20°C (68°F) to 27°C (80°F), while the evenings are deliciously refreshing.

From December to February, Cairo and the Nile see a modest dip in temperature, creating a relaxing setting for your honeymoon. This season is ideal for romantic outings such as hot air balloon rides over Luxor's stunning landscapes, marveling at the splendor of the ancient temples of Karnak and Luxor in soft, golden sunlight, or delving into the Egyptian Museum without breaking a sweat. Daytime temperatures in Cairo typically vary from 15°C (59°F) to 18°C (64°F), whereas temperatures near the Nile in Luxor range from 19°C (66°F) to 24°C (75°F). Pack light clothing for daytime exploring and heavier jackets for cold nighttime stargazing.

Spring in Egypt, which lasts from March to April, brings longer days, milder temperatures, and bright colors, making it an ideal time for a honeymoon trip. Spend your days enjoying Aswan's flowering flowers and rich botanical gardens, or take in a calm sunset over the Nile while contemplating the wonders of the ancient country. Temperatures in the Nile area normally vary from 22°C (72°F) to 30°C (86°F) throughout these months, making them ideal for outdoor sports and cultural exploration. However, be careful that the khamsin, a hot, dusty wind that may decrease vision and cause discomfort for certain

CAIRO AND THE NILE TRAVEL GUIDE

people, may arrive in April.

While Cairo and the Nile are captivating all year, the months of October to April provide the ideal combination of beautiful weather, fewer people, and amazing experiences commemorating the love that connects you and your spouse. You may relax, explore, and immerse yourself in Cairo's and the Nile region's rich historic and cultural tapestry, creating experiences that will last a lifetime. These months provide the elements for a wonderful honeymoon, resulting in an unmatched love tale imbued with Egypt's enchantment and mysticism.

CAIRO AND THE NILE ARE AT THEIR PEAK SEASON

airo and the Nile are two of Egypt's most famous
tourist spots, drawing millions of visitors from all
over the globe. It's no secret that these two locations
have an irresistible allure. Cairo and the Nile, with
their rich history, amazing architecture, and breathtaking
scenery, guarantee unique experiences for visitors. In this
chapter, we'll talk about the busiest time of year to visit
Cairo and the Nile and walk you through the finest
activities and tips to make the most of your trip.

When Is The Busiest Season?

The peak season in Egypt, which encompasses Cairo
and the Nile, often occurs between October and April.
Compared to hot summers, the temperature is cooler
and more pleasant throughout these months. The busiest
months are December and January when travelers come to
Egypt to escape the cold and bask in the warmth of the
Egyptian sun.

Why Go During The High Season?

Despite being busier and more costly, peak season has its
allure. During these months, Cairo and the Nile Valley have
various fascinating events and activities. The good weather
also lets you see historical places and landscapes without

overheating.

Attractions & Activities Not To Miss

During peak season, be sure to include the following sights and activities in your itinerary:

1. The Great Pyramids of Giza: Witness the timeless beauty of the ancient world's most intriguing buildings. While there may be more people during peak season, the milder temperatures make wandering around the pyramids much more pleasurable. Remember to take a priceless snapshot of the renowned Sphinx.

2. The Egyptian Museum: Set aside a day to study the rich history portrayed at the Egyptian Museum's large collection, which houses hundreds of items, including the famed Tutankhamun's golden death mask. During peak season, arriving early in the morning is best to avoid long lines and crowds.

3. Nile Cruises: A trip to Egypt would be completed without a Nile cruise. Travel into Egypt's core, touring ancient monuments and soaking in the timeless splendor of the Nile Valley. Booking your Nile cruise in advance is strongly advised during the peak season to guarantee you obtain your desired dates.

4. Old Cairo: Explore historic churches, mosques, and synagogues amid the meandering lanes of Old Cairo for a flavor of old-world authenticity. The features include the Hanging Church, Ibn Tulun Mosque, and Ben Ezra Synagogue. This region is less congested than other famous tourist destinations, making it ideal for exploring at your speed.

5. Temples of Luxor and Karnak: Luxor is a treasure trove for history lovers, and seeing the beautiful temples of Luxor and Karnak is an experience to be noticed. During peak season, the gigantic ancient buildings come to life with unique, breathtaking light and sound performances.

Practical Advice For The High Season

While the peak season offers a wealth of thrilling events, it is always a good idea to keep the following practical advice in mind to make the most of your trip:

1. Plan ahead of time for your flights and lodgings to ensure stable availability and pricing due to excessive demand.
2. Arrive early to avoid long lines and to handle smaller crowds while visiting famous sights.
3. bring drinks, sunscreen, and a hat to protect oneself from the Egyptian sun.
4. Expect price increases at tourist attractions; feel free to haggle with local merchants.

Finally, the peak season in Cairo and the Nile provides an unequaled experience for those looking to see Egypt's beauties. By carefully organizing your journey and keeping these key ideas in mind, you will have an outstanding trip that will leave you with memories that last a lifetime.

CAIRO AND THE NILE DURING SPRING

C airo and the Nile River awaken from their winter sleep to embrace the enticing charms of spring as the days lengthen and the temperatures begin to climb. This enthralling season adds a magical touch to Egypt's busy city and the life-giving river that passes through it, bringing colors, views, and experiences that will leave even the most seasoned tourist speechless.

A Blooming City

Spring in Cairo is a sight, with the city gently awakening under the warm Egyptian sun. Lands formerly dominated by drab and grey are now covered with magnificent blossoms. There's no doubt that Cairo in spring has an appealing charm that is genuinely tempting, whether it's the brilliant purple of the jacaranda trees, the joyful yellow of the acacia, or the sweet aroma of orange blossoms that scents the air.

As you navigate the city's busy streets, stop by public gardens like Al-Azhar Park, the Orman Botanical Garden, or the lush Gezira Island, where you can immerse yourself in a green oasis and take a stroll through beautifully landscaped spaces that offer tranquility amidst Cairo's hustle and bustle.

Serenade Of The Nile

If Cairo is Egypt's beating heart, the Nile River is its vital flowing force. The Nile's significance to Egypt cannot be emphasized, and spring is an excellent time to enjoy a leisurely sail along this ancient river. The warm air brings the musical sound of traditional Egyptian musicians playing the oud (a pear-shaped stringed instrument) as the sun sets over the Nile, creating a mystical environment that is guaranteed to capture your senses.

For a more personal and genuine Nile experience, take a traditional felucca sailboat ride during your spring visit. With their delicately arched masts and trapezoidal sails, these magnificent wooden boats have sailed the Nile's waters for decades. They will give you an up-close and personal glimpse of the river in all its springtime splendor. You'll witness fisherman throwing their nets, families picnicking on the riverbanks, and long-legged herons and egrets fishing on the shallow shoreline as you sail.

Temple And Tomb Stories

The pleasant spring weather makes it an ideal time to see the Nile Valley's many monuments, tombs, and ancient temples. Because Cairo is close to some of Egypt's most important ancient monuments, you can marvel at the splendor of the Pyramids of Giza, the Sphinx, and the Saqqara Necropolis in minutes. Temperatures in the 20-30°C (68-86°F) range make touring these great places much more bearable than in the hot summer months.

Take the chance to see Luxor and Aswan, where you may marvel at the Temple of Karnak, the Valley of the Kings, and the Philae Temple, to mention a few. The colorful wildflowers that blossom beside these ancient monuments add to the spectacular, larger-than-life pictures of gods and pharaohs that decorate these temples, providing picture-perfect recollections of your springtime excursion down the Nile.

Gastronomy And Festivities

Spring provides a fresh feeling of warmth to the weather and the Egyptian people's hearts. Celebrating the spring season is an important part of local culture, with people gathering for Sham el-Nessim, an ancient Pharaonic celebration marking the start of spring. This delightful celebration is packed with joyful reunions, outdoor picnics, and mouth-watering traditional dishes like salted fish, boiled eggs, and green onions - a one-of-a-kind gastronomic experience you won't want to miss.

Engaging your senses is an important component of travel. Cairo and the Nile in spring will captivate your eyes, ears, nose, and taste buds with their vivid colors, musical sounds, sweet smells, and delicious tastes. With so much to offer, now is the time to pack your bags and go to Egypt's capital to enjoy the majesty of the Nile River in full bloom.

SUMMER IN CAIRO AND THE NILE

The aroma of history and culture permeates the air as you travel through Cairo's busy streets toward the gleaming Nile River. Summertime in Egypt is notoriously hot, with temperatures often exceeding 40°C (104°F) in June, July, and August. However, a summer journey to Cairo and the Nile with good preparation and a sense of adventure can be an enormously rewarding and unique experience. In this chapter, we'll look at what Cairo and the Nile offer during this hot season.

Cairo, The Eternal City

Despite the heat, summer in Cairo has its distinct ambiance. The days are long and sunny, offering sufficient chance to explore the millennia-old city. Begin your day early, while the weather is cooler, with a visit to the magnificent Giza Plateau. You may see the ancient splendor of the Great Pyramids of Giza and the Sphinx from here. Hiring a qualified guide ahead of time would enhance your trip, assisting you in comprehending the importance and nuanced history of these great landmarks.

A stroll around Islamic Cairo is an essential must for history buffs. The Al-Azhar Mosque, the Sultan Hassan Mosque, and the Mosque of Ibn Tulun all have spiritual and architectural appeal. Each one weighs history inside its walls, and meandering among them is like stepping back. As the weather heats up, visit one of Cairo's many intriguing museums. The freshly built Grand Egyptian Museum offers an intriguing voyage of discovery, unraveling the secrets of ancient Egypt. Meanwhile, with its world-renowned collection of pharaoh artifacts like Tutankhamun's, the Egyptian Museum of Antiquities enables you to discover even more riches.

Treat yourself to a classic Egyptian lunch at one of Cairo's culinary treasures to beat the noon heat. At eateries like Abou Tarek or Felfela, savor wonderful dishes like koshary, molokhia, and shawarma. Alternatively, choose a modern, air-conditioned location such as Cairo Kitchen or Zooba for a more modern gourmet journey.

The Nile: A Living River

The Nile has been a lifeline for Egyptians for millennia, and a summer visit gives an ideal chance to see its magnificence. A felucca sail at sunset is one of the most peaceful ways to get acquainted with the Grand River. The exquisite, traditional wooden sailboats float elegantly over the calm waves of the Nile, relishing the peacefulness of the water and the cool evening wind.

The Nile may also be explored in a traditional dahabiya or a contemporary luxury cruise ship. Several firms provide Nile cruises, an opportunity to see Egypt's antiquities in a new light. A cruise normally takes you from Cairo (or close) to Luxor and Aswan, with captivating stops in between. These cruises guarantee that you see the most significant places while learning about their historical and cultural value, whether you pick a three-day whirlwind tour or a leisurely seven-day excursion.

Travel back in time as you explore the temples of Karnak, Luxor, Abu Simbel, Philae, and many more throughout your voyage. The diverse collection of monuments with distinct stories and styles will capture your imagination and appreciation. Remember to dress properly (in light, breathable clothes) and bring lots of sunscreens since many of these places are exposed to the elements.

Evenings Under The Stars

During the summer, Cairo's nightlife is active and diversified. Sip a refreshing mint tea at the famed El Fishawy café in the heart of Khan el-Khalili market, or see a classic Egyptian Tanoura dance performance at the Wekalet El-Ghouri Arts Center. For a more contemporary experience, visit Zamalek, an affluent neighborhood brimming with contemporary galleries, quirky bars, and world-class restaurants. You can enjoy the skyline vista and the dazzling lights reflected on the Nile from here, making it the ideal way to conclude a hot day in Cairo.

To summarize, summer in Cairo and along the Nile may be hot, but it does not diminish the enchantment of this ancient region. Cairo and the Nile offer travelers many remarkable experiences, with interesting historical monuments, delicious food, and a thriving modern culture. Bring sunscreen, remain hydrated, and enjoy your tour through time, history, and Egypt's astounding treasures.

AUTUMN IN CAIRO AND ON THE NILE

Autumn in Cairo and along the Nile is nothing short of magical, as the flaming colors of summer give way to a soothing embrace of russet tones. This season provides a mellower experience to tourists seeking an experiential trip into the heart of Egypt, offering relief from the blistering heat and bustling tourist rush.

Dive Into Cairo's Cultural Vitality

The transition of Cairo's scenery into a warm, sepia-toned fantasy is best experienced when meandering through Zamalek's tree-lined alleys or Old Cairo's twisting passageways. This is the time of year when the city's creative pulse quickens and the neighborhoods wake up to a cultural symphony. Take advantage of the colder weather to explore Downtown Cairo's urban canvas, where ancient architecture and modern murals coexist alongside lively coffee shops, galleries, and theaters.

Autumn is also festival season in Cairo, with the Cairo International Festival of Contemporary and Experimental Theatre beginning in September. This famous festival offers a bustling atmosphere for theater fans, with displays by local and worldwide performers. The Cairo International Film Festival, which takes place in November and offers a cinematic feast of regional and worldwide films, is just a little behind.

Autumn's attractiveness in Cairo is wider than its cultural offerings. The Nile's riches generate a thriving gastronomy scene celebrating Egypt's agricultural prosperity. Visit local markets, such as the Souq Al Gom'aa, to enjoy the harvest of fruits and vegetables and dates, a famous fall staple. Treat yourself to a gourmet excursion onboard a wooden felucca, sampling local cuisines as you travel down the Nile for a more luxurious experience.

By The Nile, Embracing Nature's Bounty

Beyond Cairo's busy streets, the Nile Valley in the fall is a sanctuary for explorers and nature lovers. Set off on a leisurely cruise between Luxor and Aswan, where you can take in the rich history and breathtaking scenery that unroll in front of you - with the comfortable weather as your constant companion.

See the many temples and monuments as you travel from city to city throughout the day. Thebes' UNESCO World Heritage cluster, which includes Karnak, Luxor Temple, and the Valley of the Kings, affords an incredible glimpse into the grandeur of the ancient world. The beautiful combination of flaming fall colors creates an ethereal sensation as you walk through these time-worn buildings.

The verdant expanses of the Fayoum Oasis will please adventurers seeking an authentic encounter with Egypt's natural richness. This oasis of dunes, freshwater lakes, and distinctive flora and wildlife, only a short drive from Cairo, thrives when the temperatures drop. Some must-see attractions in this off-the-beaten-path paradise are Medinet Madi's oracle temple, El-Fayoum's waterwheels, and the breathtaking Valley of the Whales.

But why limit your investigations to the ground when you can see the Nile from above? Set your aim high and reward yourself with a hot air balloon flight at dawn in Luxor. You'll be transported to a place unfettered by the time when the sun rises and shines its magical light over the colossal shapes and the shimmering Nile.

Autumn On The Nile: A Festive Season

Autumn marks the beginning of numerous important cultural and religious festivals in Egypt. Among these festivals is the Coptic Christian community's November Feast of Saint George. This yearly pilgrimage to Luxor's Coptic Monastery of Saint George provides a chance for cultural interaction and learning as people come to commemorate this venerated saint via prayers, singing, and dance.

As the season draws to a close, the Nile's banks come alive with the cacophony of the annual Waterwheel Festival, known as Qarqon El Nil. This dynamic local celebration, held around December, celebrates Nile-sourced land agriculture and is highlighted by vivid traditional music and dance performances, storytelling, and art.

Autumn along the Nile delivers many activities to suit various interests. The season provides a silently flowing symphony of color, art, and history, from the heart-stirring splendor of Cairo's cultural environment to the calm oasis of the Nile Valley. It transports you to a realm that embodies the spirit of Egypt's history, where you may breathe in the warm tones of orange and allow the city's colorful notes to fill your senses.

WINTER IN CAIRO
AND THE NILE

In the winter, Cairo and the Nile provide a fantastic chance for visitors to enjoy Egypt's beauty, history, and culture at a comfortable temperature. This chapter will guide you through the fascinating activities available during the colder months, from viewing spectacular Islamic architecture in Old Cairo to a sumptuous and relaxed Nile cruise.

The sweltering heat of summer gives way to a gentler environment when winter falls in Egypt from November to March, with temperatures ranging from 15 to 25 degrees Celsius (59 to 77 degrees Fahrenheit). This break from the heat is ideal for exploring Cairo's busy streets, delving into its ancient history, and meandering along the Nile's banks.

Cairo: A City Rich In History

Cairo, also known as the City of a Thousand Minarets, will wow you with its magnificent architectural treasures, rich history, and active local culture. The Citadel of Salah el-Din, a historic stronghold with panoramic city views, is a must-see during the winter. The neighboring Muhammad Ali Mosque is a stunning example of Ottoman architecture, and the colder temperature allows for leisurely investigation.

Continue your tour through Coptic Cairo's small lanes, a

unique neighborhood merging ancient churches, Roman ruins, and vibrant local life. The winter months are ideal for exploring the rebuilt Ben Ezra Synagogue and the Hanging Church without fighting crowds.

Winter is also a great time to visit the Egyptian Museum, where you can spend hours gazing at pharaonic artifacts, like the famed Tutankhamun display, without being suffocated by the summer heat. Visit the contemporary Grand Egyptian Museum, which opened in 2021 and has since grown to become the world's biggest archaeological museum.

A Nile Adventure

The cooler temperature makes sailing on the Nile very appealing, and several classic sailing boats, known as feluccas, are available for hire at low costs. Take a sunset ride down the Nile, seeing local life along the riverbanks, an experience enhanced by the peacefulness of the winter air. Now is also an excellent time to visit the many riverbank parks and cafés, such as Darb 1718, a cultural hub with frequent exhibitions and seminars.

Luxor And Aswan: Exploring The Ancient World

Travel beyond Cairo to Luxor and Aswan's ancient wonders for a stunning winter vacation. Sail downstream in the fresh air on a sumptuous Nile cruise, a classic Egyptian experience, passing through the beautiful vistas of the Nile Valley. Explore the temples of Karnak and Luxor along the journey, where the painted columns and sculptures are even more vibrant in the colder months.

A more peaceful and pleasant ambiance, coupled with the soothing beat of the Nile, awaits in Aswan. Aswan, being farther south, is somewhat warmer even in winter. The Old Dam, the Unfinished Obelisk, and the beautiful Temple of Isis on Philae Island are among the city's most notable landmarks. During your visit, immerse yourself in the colorful Nubian culture by wandering around the bustling villages, feasting on traditional foods, and experiencing their traditional hospitality.

Winter in Cairo and the Nile provides an unparalleled experience for those looking to see Egypt's rich history, lively culture, and timeless beauty. A voyage down the Nile and into the heart of Cairo will capture the hearts of those lucky enough to experience it, with milder temperatures, fewer people, and stunning vistas.

A MONTH-BY-MONTH ITINERARY FOR EXPLORING CAIRO AND THE NILE

Cairo and the Nile, Egypt's heart, give tourists an enriching and exhilarating experience waiting to be discovered. The unlimited array of cultural, historical, and natural features combine with the desert region's distinct ambiance to create a memorable experience. Because each month adds a unique charm to this gorgeous location, this chapter will guide you through selecting the best time to visit Cairo and the Nile.

January: A Cool Start

The beginning of the year brings colder temperatures but bright and sunny days, with average temperatures of 16°C (61°F). January is great for seeing Cairo's prominent monuments, from the Great Pyramids to busy markets. The Egyptian Museum houses a massive collection of ancient antiquities and is also a must-see this month.

February Is The Month Of Love

For all the romantics, February is a perfect time to visit Cairo and the Nile. Mild weather makes it an ideal month for a leisurely exploration of the city, with botanical gardens in full bloom and lovebirds coming to the island of Gezira to take in the scenery. Furthermore, your vacation would be complete once you walked down the Nile promenade or dined at a beautiful riverfront restaurant.

March: Spring Celebrations

As spring approaches, Cairo comes alive with the blossoming of flowers and a slew of events. March brings tourists a moderate and pleasant temperature ideal for felucca sailing on the Nile. You may also join the locals in celebrating Sham el-Nessim, an ancient Egyptian celebration held on the first day of spring.

Embracing The Warmth In April

With rising temperatures, April is ideal for outdoor activities such as golfing and sunbathing in the several luxury resorts surrounding Cairo. However, it is crucial to remember that the prevalence of desert sandstorms known as "khamsin" may influence vision and air quality throughout this month.

May Is A Month Full Of Sun And Fun.

The city grows hotter in May, yet the celebrations continue. This month features events, including the International Arabian Horse Championships and the annual Ramadan Lanterns Festival. The daytime heat may be oppressive, but it ensures enjoyable nights exploring Cairo's nightlife at pubs and clubs.

June: Nile Evenings And Desert Heat

Egypt is hot in June, often topping 35°C (95°F). Consequently, it's best to plan your activities around bodies of water. You may escape the desert heat by visiting the Mediterranean coast or taking an evening Nile boat to see Cairo's lit skyline after sunset.

July Is The Hottest Month Of The Year.

July is the hottest month of the year, with oppressively high temperatures. The variety of activities accessible surrounding the Nile, on the other hand, might give some reprieve for tourists during this month. The International Nile Song Festival, a multicultural festival showcasing music from diverse parts of the Nile Basin, is one such activity.

August: Cultural Encounters In The Heat

Travelers that can tolerate hot temperatures may enjoy the Egyptian cultural experience in August. Many museums provide entry discounts, and many courses and activities center on the country's ancient past, ranging from pottery-making to hieroglyphics studies.

September: A Glorious Art Oasis

This month, Cairo hosts the International Biennale of Contemporary Art, a world-renowned contemporary art festival that shows the works of both new and recognized artists worldwide. The milder weather in September is also ideal for outdoor exploration and city strolls.

Al-Mawlid Al-Nabawi, October

October marks the great Islamic holiday of Al-Mawlid Al-Nabawi, which celebrates the Prophet Muhammad's birthday and is temporarily cooler than previous summer months. This season, Cairo is brimming with remarkable religious and cultural activities, offering an enlightening tour for religious and secular guests.

The Ultimate Cultural Escape In November

With rising temperatures, November is perfect for seeing the city's historic attractions. To escape the hot summer heat, visit the Giza Plateau, home to the Great Sphinx and the Pyramids, this month.

A Pharaonic Farewell In December

December allows travelers to complete their trip in Egypt's unique cultural environment. Cairo enthusiastically welcomes both the ancient and the modern, giving visitors a feeling of the tremendous sweep of time and history that creates this magnificent metropolis, with the city draped in festive lights to greet the new year.

While each month brings a unique flavor to Cairo and the Nile area, your particular tastes and intended activities ultimately determine the ideal time to come. Regardless of when you come, the rich history, culture, and stunning natural beauty of Cairo and the Nile will leave you with unforgettable memories.

CAIRO AND THE NILE TRAVEL ESSENTIALS

The ever-changing temperature, cultural customs, and diverse range of activities available might make planning a vacation to this wonderful area seem daunting. However, with these Cairo and Nile packing requirements, you'll be properly prepared for your Egyptian journey.

Clothing

Egypt's climate varies tremendously depending on the season and where you are along the Nile. Cairo generally has hot, dry summers and pleasant winters, with the Nile area being significantly hotter. As a result, choosing lightweight, breathable clothes is preferable. Linen, cotton, and moisture-wicking materials should be wardrobe staples.

Dress modestly to respect Egypt's largely Muslim culture. Covering the shoulders, chest, and knees is particularly important while visiting religious buildings such as mosques. A shawl or scarf to cover your head in more conservative regions or religious locations is essential for ladies. Long pants or knee-length shorts are recommended for men.

Pack the following essential clothing items:

1. Loose-fitting trousers or skirts - Keep cool by

wearing lightweight, full-length bottoms that follow local conventions.

2. Long-sleeved shirts or blouses - Choose breathable materials to protect your skin from the sun and mosquitoes while being culturally acceptable.

3. A light jacket or cardigan - Evening temperatures in Cairo and near the Nile may be cold, so a light layer for warmth is recommended.

4. Comfortable, durable shoes are necessary for touring, strolling, and seeing historic sites.

5. Sunglasses and a wide-brimmed hat - These essentials will shade your eyes from the bright sunlight while protecting your face and neck from dangerous UV radiation.

Medicine And Medical Supplies

Comprehensive travel insurance is highly advised to guarantee you have access to competent healthcare services in the event of an emergency.

Pack the following items to prevent any unforeseen health issues:

1. Your first-aid box should include Band-aids, pain relievers, anti-diarrhea medicine, antihistamines, and any prescription medication you need.

2. Insect repellent - Because the Nile is known for mosquitoes, invest in a high-quality mosquito repellent to keep those annoying insects at bay.

3. Sunscreen - Sun protection is essential, particularly if you want to spend time outside seeing ancient monuments or boating down the Nile.

4. Hand sanitizer - Maintaining excellent hygiene when traveling is critical, especially in countries with limited

clean running water.

5. Water purification pills or a portable water filter - It's important to remain hydrated before beginning your Egyptian adventure, but tap water may be unsafe to drink. To guarantee safe drinking water, use purification pills or a filter.

Electronic Gadgets

1. Egypt employs a variety of power outlets, so invest in a high-quality universal adaptor that can accommodate numerous plug kinds.
2. With potentially long travel days and limited access to power outlets, having your own portable charger may be a lifesaver.
3. Camera or smartphone with a dependable camera - Capture unforgettable images of Egypt's stunning beauty to remember your thrilling adventures.

Document Requirements

Aside from keeping your passport, airline tickets, and other travel or visa paperwork safe and organized, having digital or paper duplicates of these materials on hand is a good idea. Bring a list of important names, phone numbers, and addresses in case of an emergency.

Packing Suggestions

1. Organize your possessions using packing cubes to make finding certain items in your suitcase easier without having to search high and low.
2. Use a day bag or backpack - A lightweight and useful bag is great for everyday travel when your wallet, passport, water bottle, and camera need quick access.

3. Pack light and practical - Overpacking may make your trips difficult, so prioritize necessary goods and restrict your baggage to one compact suitcase or backpack.

Finally, your Cairo and Nile packing requirements will set the tone for a pleasant, wonderful vacation. You'll be well-equipped to discover Egypt's rich history and enchanting beauty with an emphasis on lightweight, modest attire, vital health supplies, and relevant travel papers.

WHAT TO PACK FOR
A NILE AND CAIRO
VACATION

A trip to Cairo and the Nile is an encounter with history, a look into the realm of the Pharaohs, and a chance to see Egypt's mysterious treasures. Preparing for such a vacation is more than simply packing your luggage; it is an important component of creating a pleasant and memorable experience. In this chapter, we'll review some essential goods to bring while going on an adventure of a lifetime.

First and foremost, while arranging a vacation to Cairo and the Nile, attire is an important concern. Egypt's climate is mostly hot and bright, with milder nights in the colder months of November and February. Pack lightweight, breathable clothing, such as cotton or linen, and comfortable walking shoes or sandals. Dress modestly for temple and mosque visits by covering your shoulders and legs, and carry a lightweight scarf to cover your hair if necessary.

Wear sunglasses, a wide-brimmed hat, and sunscreen to protect yourself from the intense Egyptian sun. Ensure your sunscreen has a wide spectrum SPF of at least 30, and remember to reapply it often throughout your activities. A tiny, foldable umbrella may be useful not just for shade but also for catching a raindrop or covering your shoulders if you need more modesty.

It's critical to remain hydrated when touring the ancient treasures. Bring a reusable water bottle to refill at your accommodation, or buy clean, filtered water from local stores. It is important to avoid drinking Egyptian tap water since it may contain germs and parasites that may cause disease. Bring a water purification solution or personal water filter as an added precaution.

Because cash transactions are still frequent in Egypt, carry a cache of tiny notes and coins for tipping and local market purchases. Furthermore, only have a little cash on you to reduce hazards. Packing a money belt or a neck pouch to keep your cash, passport, and other critical papers secure while visiting the region is also a good idea.

Electronics like your smartphone and camera are crucial for recording memories and navigating Cairo and the Nile. Pack a portable charger, extra batteries, and plug adapters for Egypt (type C and F plugs with two round pins) to get the most out of them. Bring a tiny notepad and pen to note important information, such as addresses or phone numbers.

Although Cairo and other major tourist locations are secure, a modest travel first aid pack is always handy. Bandages, antiseptic wipes, pain remedies, rehydration salts, and any prescription drugs you may need should be included. Pack bug repellant since mosquitoes may be a problem near the Nile.

An excellent guidebook is essential for capturing the splendor of Cairo and the Nile. Invest in a current version with full maps, historical background, and suggestions for real, local experiences. Furthermore, installing offline maps and language translation applications on your smartphone might be a lifeline throughout your vacation.

Finally, bring a modest assortment of snacks or energy bars to keep you going on lengthy hikes. While Egyptian food is excellent and satisfying, local alternatives may be limited as you go farther up the Nile.

You'll be well-equipped with these goods in your suitcase to make your Cairo and Nile holiday delightful and memorable. Embrace the thrill and immerse yourself in this intriguing land's rich history and culture, knowing that you are well-prepared for what lies ahead.

THE MOST USEFUL ITEMS

Having the appropriate stuff in your baggage may make or break your Egyptian excursion, guaranteeing a smooth and pleasant journey. This section of the travel guide delves into the most useful things to carry with you while you experience the attractions of Cairo and the Nile.

Clothing For The Weather

It is important to consider the weather in Egypt when packing your baggage. The weather is often hot and dry during the day but chilly at night. Cotton and linen are lightweight, light-colored, and breathable materials suitable for daytime wear in Cairo. Visitors should dress comfortably and modestly when visiting religious places such as mosques. Women should bring a lightweight scarf to conceal their hair in such areas. A simple jacket or sweater should keep you warm and comfy on nights boating the Nile.

Comfortable Footwear

With its lively streets and interesting sights, Cairo necessitates a lot of walking. Shoes that are both comfortable and strong are essential for touring the Pyramids of Giza, the Egyptian Museum, and exploring the intriguing streets of Old Cairo. Sandals or flip-flops are perfect for a stroll down the Nile or resting aboard your Nile cruise.

Sun Protection

The Egyptian sun is not underestimated, particularly when spending a long time outside. To protect your skin and eyes from dangerous ultraviolet (UV) radiation, wear high-quality sunglasses, a wide-brimmed hat, and sunscreen with a high SPF. Remember to reapply sunscreen frequently, and consider taking an umbrella for further protection from the scorching heat.

Snacks And Hydration

It's critical to remain hydrated when visiting Cairo and the Nile. Carrying a reusable water bottle allows you to stay hydrated without adversely hurting the environment. While sipping water, chew on nutritious foods like dried fruits, almonds, or energy bars. These will satisfy your appetite and supply you with the energy you need to explore Egypt's wonders.

Essentials Of Health And Sanitation

A modest package of basic first aid goods is usually useful when traveling. Band-aids, pain remedies, motion sickness medicine, and any recommended medication should be included. Furthermore, hand sanitizers and wet wipes come in helpful while exploring Cairo and the Nile, where clean water may not always be readily accessible for washing your hands or cleaning up after an accident.

Electronics And Networking

Electronics play an important part in contemporary travel, from snapping the ideal image of the Sphinx to keeping connected with loved ones at home. Portable power banks, universal travel adaptors, and a decent camera or smartphone are essential. Staying connected is often made simple by local SIM cards that provide reasonable data packages and are readily bought at Cairo's airport or city hubs.

Finally, remember to bring a feeling of adventure and curiosity. With these essentials in your suitcase, you'll be well-equipped to immerse yourself in the enthralling world of Cairo and the Nile, making memories that last a lifetime.

IS IT SAFE TO GO TO CAIRO OR THE NILE?

airo, Egypt's capital and home to the magnificent Great Pyramids of Giza and the Sphinx, has captured the minds of visitors from all over the globe. The magnificent Nile, which cradles the country's rich history, adds to the attractiveness of this wonderful place. But, if you're thinking of visiting Cairo and the Nile, the first thing that comes to mind is safety.

Cairo's security

Regarding safety, Cairo has had its fair share of ups and downs. However, the Egyptian government has significantly improved security measures surrounding the city and its tourist sites in recent years. Cairo is now largely regarded as secure for visitors, as seen by the rising number of tourists visiting the city in recent years.

Taking conventional measures while traveling to a large city such as Cairo is important. Be aware of your surroundings and monitor your personal things, especially in busy places like marketplaces. Petty theft is possible in every major city, but being careful and vigilant may considerably lower the danger.

Cairo's crowded, chaotic streets and sometimes informal traffic restrictions may make road safety a struggle. Crossing roadways should be done with extreme caution as a pedestrian. Prepare to negotiate a tangle of automobiles,

GENEVA WALKER

people, and the odd animal while driving. Many visitors may find hiring a local driver more convenient or using trustworthy taxi and ride-hailing services.

Along the Nile, there is safety.
Cruising along the Nile is vital to every Egyptian vacation, providing breathtaking vistas of historic monuments, lush green landscapes, and active communities. Security has been beefed up along the river, especially in popular tourist destinations like Luxor and Aswan. For this reason, enjoying a Nile cruise is typically seen as risk-free.

It is essential, however, to choose a reputable and licensed tour operator who will prioritize your safety and follow government safety standards. Choosing a reputable operator guarantees your experience is both pleasurable and safe.

Hygiene and health
Maintaining excellent health and cleanliness is critical when visiting Cairo and the Nile. Tourists may occasionally encounter food and water-borne diseases, but by taking precautions, you may reduce your risk.

Drink only bottled or filtered water and avoid using ice in drinks. For street food, seek sellers who prepare the dish before you. Consuming undercooked or non-peelable fruits and vegetables should be avoided since contamination is risky.

Furthermore, before your trip, see your doctor or a travel health center for professional guidance on vaccines and other health measures.

Terrorism and political stability
Egypt has previously suffered political instability

104

and terrorist concerns. However, the situation has substantially improved over the years due to the government's strengthened security measures. Tourist sites in Cairo and along the Nile are typically considered safe, but it's critical to remain current on your country's travel recommendations.

To summarize, although no place can guarantee complete safety, your vacation to Cairo and the Nile may be a genuinely amazing and secure experience if you take the necessary measures and thoroughly study. You may completely immerse yourself in the enchanting sights and sounds that have made Egypt a favorite among travelers worldwide by remaining knowledgeable about local legislation, interacting with reliable operators, and sticking to health, hygiene, and safety precautions.

SUGGESTIONS FOR BEING SAFE IN CAIRO AND ALONG THE NILE

H istorically and culturally rich, Cairo and the Nile draw millions of tourists each year. Egypt's scenery and people are undeniably appealing, but there are certain safety risks that all visitors should be aware of to properly enjoy their experiences. This chapter focuses on practical safety and security considerations while touring Cairo and the Nile.

Cairo is well-known for its hectic traffic. Take additional precautions while crossing streets or traveling around the city. It is critical to be awake and aware of your surroundings. When possible, utilize approved pedestrian crossings and footbridges.

Petty Theft And Pickpocketing

Pickpocketing and petty theft are common targets for tourists. Keep your valuables close at hand and think about utilizing theft-proof purses or money belts. Be careful with your possessions in busy settings such as bazaars or public transit. You should also divide your cash and credit cards to have a backup in case anything goes wrong.

Transportation

Regarding local transportation, get to know reliable

providers and kinds of transit. To prevent overpricing scams, use legal white taxis with meters or well-rated ride-hailing services like Uber. Take care of your baggage and keep it visible by bus or rail traveling.

The Dress Code

Dressing modestly will demonstrate respect for local customs and traditions and assist you in blending in more readily. Both men and women should avoid wearing exposing or tight clothing. When visiting sacred locations, women should bring a lightweight scarf to cover their shoulders and neck.

Scams

Scams may happen everywhere, but travelers should be especially wary of excessively nice people or unsolicited aid offers. Be wary of anybody who insists on giving you a present since it may come with an expectation of payment. Do careful study and obtain suggestions from reliable sources, other tourists, or your hotel's front desk before purchasing any trips or merchandise.

Hygiene And Health

Always put your health first by practicing proper hygiene and consuming nutritious meals. Stick to properly prepared meals and bottled or purified water, and avoid street food sellers. To reduce the risk of infection, have hand sanitizer and disinfectant wipes on hand. Before you go, check with your doctor about any required immunizations or prescriptions.

Photography

While snapping photographs is a vital aspect of traveling, it is also crucial to be courteous. Avoid photographing military, police, or government institutions since this may result in difficulties. Always get permission before photographing individuals since only some enjoy being photographed.

Cultural Awareness

Being culturally aware may help to defuse potentially dangerous situations. Learn about local traditions and manners to show respect and prevent accidentally upsetting someone. Egyptians are typically kind and inviting, and they will appreciate your attempts to learn about their culture.

Protests Against Politics

Avoid regions where there is political instability or demonstrations. You may unwittingly get involved in a stressful scenario as a foreign tourist. It is critical to remain current on the latest developments and follow the advice issued by your embassy or consulate.

Nile Cruising Security

Cruising the Nile River is a memorable experience, but choosing a reputable cruise operator with enough safety precautions is important. Check that your chosen boat has life jackets, fire extinguishers, and a well-trained crew. Remember to notify relatives and friends of your itinerary and the cruise line's contact information.

To summarize, keeping safe in Cairo and the Nile requires being alert, aware, and courteous. Following these suggestions will help you make the most of your vacation and create lasting memories of your wonderful Egyptian journey.

IS CAIRO AND THE NILE SAFE AT NIGHT?

When considering touring Cairo and the Nile, you may be concerned about the region's safety, particularly at night. This chapter will illuminate several evening safety issues in Cairo and along the Nile.

Cairo is a vibrant metropolis with over 20 million people and many cultural and historical attractions. Its inhabitants are known for their kindness and hospitality. Recognizing the significance of tourism to Egypt's economy, the Egyptian government has spent enormous resources in recent years to ensure tourists feel comfortable and secure throughout their stay.

Cairo and the Nile are generally safe at night, provided basic safety measures are followed and local traditions and customs are respected. As a precaution, authorities have strengthened their security presence, particularly at important tourist destinations. Nonetheless, being alert to your surroundings and trusting your senses is critical.

Public And Tourist Areas Should Be Safe.

Most tourist locations in Cairo, like Tahrir Square, the Khan El-Khalili Bazaar, and Zamalek, are quite safe to visit at night. Popular tourist destinations along the Nile River, such as Luxor and Aswan, have also increased security, with several patrols and checkpoints in place to safeguard the safety of both residents and tourists.

However, staying close to the major tourist places and avoiding dark or lonely alleyways is still best. Stick to populated and known districts, and double-check landmark visitation hours, since certain sites may be closed at night.

Transportation Security

Choose safe and dependable transportation alternatives while you're at night. Taxis, Uber, and Careem (a local ride-hailing service) are all regarded as safe ways to navigate Cairo at night. Before using public transportation, confirm the specifics with your hotel or tour operator since not all forms of transportation are well-maintained or provide nighttime service.

Travelers traveling along the Nile are also advised to schedule a Nile Cruise or Felucca ride with reliable tour operators to assure their safety and comfort on the water.

Etiquette And Cultural Sensitivity

Egypt is a largely Muslim nation, so learning the local traditions and using common sense while interacting with the locals may go a long way toward guaranteeing your safety. It is important to dress modestly in public, observe religious rituals, and avoid too affectionate shows.

Scams And Minor Crimes

While crime in Cairo and along the Nile is relatively minimal, it is always prudent to remain wary of pickpockets, particularly in busy marketplaces and tourist areas. Carry your luggage and valuables securely, and avoid flaunting costly items, jewelry, or large sums of money.

Tourist scams may also occur, such as unsolicited offers for guided tours or locals insisting on assisting you in finding your way about only to demand money afterward. In these cases, it is essential to gently and firmly deny their services.

Cairo and the Nile are unquestionably attractive and enthralling places to explore during the day and at night. Visitors may enjoy the beauty and history of this unique place without fear if they take a responsible approach to safety and respect local traditions. Maintain your vigilance, trust your instincts, and enjoy the amazing experience of Cairo and the Nile.

IS IT SAFE FOR A SINGLE FEMALE TO VISIT CAIRO AND THE NILE?

A s a solitary female tourist in this North African city, you may be concerned about your safety and cultural standards. In this chapter, we will address these issues and provide helpful recommendations to guarantee that you have a pleasant and safe time while seeing Cairo and the Nile.

Safety is a legitimate worry for any visitor. Still, it is important to know that the hazards you encounter in Cairo are not unlike those in other big cities across the globe. Egypt has taken great measures to strengthen security in recent years, particularly in tourist regions. The police presence has increased, and there has been significant investment in infrastructure and services to boost tourism. To protect your safety, however, it is still important to be educated, be alert of your surroundings, and take simple measures.

Unwanted attention is a prevalent problem for female tourists in Cairo, and it may take the form of staring, catcalling, or even groping. These occurrences may be frightening and draining, but staying strong and aggressive in your response is key. Always follow your instincts; if you feel uneasy, find a method to get out of the situation. Dressing modestly by covering your shoulders, chest, and knees and wearing sunglasses to minimize eye contact may help decrease unwanted attention. It's crucial to remember that these instances are more likely in crowded settings or on public transportation, so try to avoid them if possible.

Navigating Cairo's busy streets may be an experience in and of itself. As a solitary female traveler, opportunistic merchants or locals may approach you for unwanted help. While many of these contacts are well-intentioned, it is critical to create boundaries to prevent anybody from taking advantage of your generosity. A strong 'no, thank you' in Arabic (la, shukran) frequently suffices. Contact security guards, female sellers, or families when seeking assistance.

The highlight of most Egyptian trips is exploring Cairo's plethora of ancient ruins and historical landmarks. Joining guided tours as a lone traveler is a fantastic opportunity to experience these places while enjoying the companionship of other travelers and the advice of competent guides. If you want to explore independently, always do your homework and consider hiring a reliable, certified tour via your hotel or a travel agency.

Regarding lodging, research is essential for a solitary female traveler. Read reviews from other tourists and favor well-known hotels or guesthouses that have received excellent comments. To save time on travel, choose a hotel in a safe area near tourist attractions. Once you've decided on a place to stay, notify a trustworthy friend or family member back home.

The Nile is an attraction in and of itself, and taking a boat along its banks is an excellent opportunity to appreciate its tranquil splendor. For the ideal cruise experience, choose a reputed cruise line and study reviews from previous passengers. Many Nile cruises provide group excursions to surrounding temples, ancient sites, and local towns, which may give company and safety in numbers for solitary female visitors.

It would help if you did not let safety fears keep you from enjoying the allure of Cairo and the Nile. You may have a wonderful tour through this fascinating place if you are aware, prepared, and take basic measures. Egypt's people are truly kind and accommodating, and they are eager for tourists to enjoy their rich culture and history. Accept this invitation and go on a once-in-a-lifetime journey as a solitary female traveler in Cairo and along the Nile.

SCAMS ON THE NILE AND IN CAIRO

As with any major tourist destination, the odd person will attempt to make quick cash from unwary travelers. This section of your travel guide will lead you through the often murky waters of scams in Cairo and along the Nile, assisting you in identifying and avoiding them while making the most of your stay in this magnificent part of the globe.

When visiting Egypt, getting acquainted with the local currency, the Egyptian Pound (EGP), is important. To prevent misunderstanding, keep up with the current conversion rates and understand the denominations of Egyptian banknotes and coins. Currency scams are common in Cairo and the Nile, with some visitors being handed counterfeit notes, overcharged, or tricked by unscrupulous money changers. It is best to receive Egyptian cash from official sources such as banks and ATMs rather than from black market operations, which may not have ethical procedures.

Surprising "Guides" and Aggressive Sales Techniques

Prepare to be approached by locals when wandering around Cairo's vivid, busy streets or admiring the Nile's myriad beauties. While Egyptians are famed for their friendliness and hospitality, some sadly seek to take advantage of visitors in a variety of ways. One such strategy is to serve as an impromptu "guide" or "friend," offering to show you around or give you instructions. In many situations, these people are looking for cash or baksheesh (a gratuity) for their uninvited services. It's essential to gently but assertively deny such offers with a strong "la shukran" (no, thank you).

Scams in Shopping and Bazaars

Cairo and the Nile are filled with vibrant bazaars, marketplaces, and souvenir stores offering anything from handmade carpets to antique relics. Not every good, however, is real. To get the most out of your shopping experience, be careful when buying high-priced things or antiques; many of these items may be convincing forgeries. When in doubt, seek the advice of an official, certified tour guide who can assist you in identifying genuine products.

Expensive Rides

Visiting Cairo and the Nile is only possible by taking a cab, tuk-tuk (auto-rickshaw), or felucca (traditional wooden sailboat). One of the most common frauds, however, includes transportation. Before hopping in a taxi or consenting to a tuk-tuk or felucca trip, be sure to negotiate a reasonable charge beforehand or, preferably, select a service that uses a meter or a set rate card. In such instances, the Uber, Careem, or Ousta app, which provides fixed rates before your travel, might be handy.

Inflation of Prices

Egyptians are skilled salesmen in addition to their warmth and friendliness. Indeed, when a visitor is recognized, Cairo is renowned for charging exorbitant fees for products and services. It is vital to haggle and negotiate pricing at marketplaces, bazaars, and taxi drivers while conducting business. A reasonable starting point is to offer half the first stated price and proceed. Also, understanding a little Arabic or soliciting the assistance of a native may help you get good deals.

Despite these possible risks, a trip to Cairo and the Nile is a once-in-a-lifetime event that an opportunistic fraudster should not ruin. With this book and a healthy dose of common sense and prudence, you may confidently tour Egypt's wonders, enhancing your experience and making amazing memories.

WHAT TO DO IN
THE EVENT OF AN
EMERGENCY

A s appealing as these areas may be, there may be times when you must cope with an emergency. In this tutorial, we'll lead you through the necessary actions and measures for dealing with an emergency while traveling, whether linked to health, security, or nature.

Emergencies In Medicine:

Anticipating and reacting to health crises is critical in Cairo, as in any major city. In such cases, knowing where to find medical services and understanding the healthcare system may make a big difference. Despite Egypt's improving healthcare system, there are great private hospitals and clinics in Cairo.

First and foremost, always have a modest first-aid kit and any essential personal medicine with you. Learn the locations of neighboring hospitals and pharmacies, and have the contact information for your embassy or consulate handy in case of a medical emergency.

Call the national emergency number at 123 if you need urgent medical help. This call will link you to an ambulance service that will take you to the closest hospital. Remember that you may need to fund ambulance expenses, so always have extra cash on you. Having full travel and medical insurance while visiting Cairo and the Nile area is essential since medical expenditures might be prohibitively expensive.

Emergencies In Security:

Though crime statistics in Cairo are lower than in other major cities, visitors should take personal safety seriously. The national police emergency number is 122 in the event of a security emergency. If you face any problems, contact the local authorities, the embassy, or the consulate immediately.

Registering your trip details with your embassy or consulate upon arrival is recommended. This informs your government of your location and allows them to contact you during a crisis. They can also advise on security precautions and issue travel recommendations based on nationality.

Maintain vigilance and awareness of your surroundings, especially in congested tourist places. Petty crime, such as pickpocketing and purse snatching, is frequent, so keep your items safe and avoid flaunting valuable jewelry, devices, or large sums of money.

Natural Disasters And Environmental Disasters:

Although Cairo and the Nile are largely protected from natural catastrophes, it is essential to be prepared for future environmental crises. Sandstorms are possible, particularly during the transitional seasons of winter to spring and summer to fall. Because these storms may have serious consequences for health and transportation, it's critical to keep informed by following local news or getting information from your embassy or consulate.

In a sandstorm, take cover immediately or protect your face and breathe via a mask or a damp towel. Avoid needless travel and stay put until the storm passes. Drink lots of water to stay hydrated and wash out any dangerous particles you may have ingested.

Traveling has inherent dangers. However, being prepared considerably reduces the likelihood of facing an emergency. Take the appropriate measures and ensure easy access to important information and connections. You'll be better prepared to manage crises throughout your Cairo and Nile journey if you plan, keep educated, and exercise prudence.

INSURANCE FOR TRAVEL SAFETY

This thrilling adventure has hazards and uncertainties, ranging from health issues to unexpected cancellations and delays. In such cases, travel protection insurance serves as a safety net, ensuring you are adequately protected against unforeseen accidents during your vacation.

When arranging a vacation to Cairo and the Nile, you should concentrate on the exciting features, such as breathtaking pyramids, busy marketplaces, and tranquil Nile cruises. However, being prepared for unexpected roadblocks is just as vital. Here are some of the reasons why purchasing travel protection insurance might be beneficial:

1. Health and Medical Emergencies: The exotic locations of Cairo and the Nile may cause health dangers. Unfamiliar locations, climate change, and risky behaviors contribute to health problems. In the event of an emergency, having comprehensive travel protection insurance guarantees that you have access to the finest medical treatment and emergency help.

2. Cancellations and Delays: Life is unpredictable, and many unanticipated events, such as sickness, job loss, or natural catastrophes, may demand adjustments in your trip arrangements. A well-designed travel protection insurance coverage will account for these risks and

give cash compensation for any cancellations or delays, assisting you in avoiding significant losses.

3. Personal Belongings Loss or Theft: No matter how cautious you are, there is always the possibility of losing your luggage or being a victim of theft when traveling, whether in the magnificent temples of Luxor, the busy streets of Cairo, or on a tranquil Nile cruise. Travel protection insurance provides financial help to replace lost or stolen possessions in the case of an unanticipated occurrence.

4. Legal and liability coverage: Travelers may encounter legal problems in other nations. From accidents and injuries to property damage, travel protection insurance may shield you from unanticipated legal responsibilities while offering access to local legal counsel if necessary.

Selecting The Best Travel Protection Insurance

Getting the correct insurance coverage that fully covers your travel demands is essential to guarantee a worry-free vacation. Here are some things to think about when choosing a travel protection insurance package:

1. Coverage depending on the location, activities, and itinerary: Consider the specific risks of your trip to Cairo and the Nile and the activities you have planned, and make a list of probable uncertainties that may develop during your travel.

2. Prioritize an insurance policy with substantial medical coverage, such as hospitalization, repatriation, and emergency help services.

3. Customizable add-ons: Select a flexible travel protection insurance package that enables you to add certain coverages depending on your trip requirements, such as extreme sports coverage, cruise protection, or rental vehicle insurance.

4. Reliable insurance provider: Compare coverage, prices, and customer reviews from several insurance companies to get a policy that is both dependable and practical.

While the draw of Cairo and the Nile may tempt you to abandon prudence, don't underestimate the necessity of being prepared for unexpected events. By purchasing appropriate travel protection insurance, you may not only secure a trouble-free vacation but also get peace of mind and concentrate on creating amazing experiences that will last a lifetime.

PLACES TO STAY IN CAIRO AND ALONG THE NILE

F inding the ideal hotel should be at the top of your agenda as you prepare to explore the city's historical attractions and immerse yourself in its lively local life. This chapter digs into the many lodgings available in Cairo and the Nile area, assisting you in making the best option for a wonderful stay.

Cairo's Deluxe Accommodations

If luxury is your primary goal, Cairo has numerous top-tier hotels that will meet your needs. These hotels provide an opulent experience thanks to their great service, world-class facilities, and prominent locations.

The Four Seasons Hotel Cairo at Nile Plaza, situated on the Nile's banks, offers breathtaking river views and convenient access to downtown Cairo. This hotel has magnificent suites, many good dining choices, a revitalizing spa, and an outdoor pool that provides the ideal setting for leisure.

The Ritz-Carlton Cairo, situated near Tahrir Square, is another premium alternative. The luxurious rooms, suites, and meticulously kept historical items in the hotel's rich surroundings display contemporary and heritage characteristics. The Egyptian Museum, which is nearby, enables you to dive into the country's ancient history at your leisure.

Cairo's Mid-Range Accommodations

Cairo boasts many mid-range hotels that provide comfort and convenience for visitors looking for a pleasant and cheap stay.

The Steigenberger El Tahrir, situated in the city center, has a modern design and a variety of basic services. The hotel is conveniently located near historic sights like the Egyptian Museum and the busy Khan el-Khalili Bazaar.

Maadi Hotel, located in the calmer Maadi district, provides a more serene retreat from the city's rush and bustle. This hotel offers big rooms, a magnificent patio overlooking the Nile, and convenient access to the downtown area by the neighboring Metro.

Cairo's Budget And Boutique Hotels

Cairo's lively downtown also offers a wealth of low-cost alternatives and boutique hotels for the discriminating tourist who appreciates both affordability and character.

Boutique hotels like the Talisman Hotel de Charme and Villa Belle Époque are ideal for individuals looking for something different and personal. These wonderfully designed resorts radiate charm and provide individual attention, allowing you to immerse yourself in a genuine Egyptian experience.

Budget options such as the Australian and Brothers Hostels are popular with backpackers and guests wishing to save money without compromising comfort. These establishments provide clean, comfortable

CAIRO AND THE NILE TRAVEL GUIDE

accommodations, a welcoming ambiance, and great positions near Cairo's main attractions.

Following The Nile River

A vacation by the Nile River allows you to experience Egyptian life at a slower, more peaceful pace. For example, Luxor and Aswan provide many hotels that enable you to bask in the region's splendor while seeing its ancient monuments.

Consider the world-renowned Sofitel Winter Palace or the Nile-front Sonesta St. George Hotel in Luxor. These hotels provide a wonderful stay due to their gorgeous architecture, superb service, and closeness to historic landmarks such as the Valley of the Kings and Karnak Temple.

In Aswan, choices range from luxurious establishments like the Old Cataract Hotel, which has hosted celebrities like Agatha Christie, to lovely guesthouses like Bet el Kerem and the Nubian-style Anakato Nubian Houses. The diverse designs and pricing range appeal to various tastes, offering an enjoyable vacation.

Finally, Cairo and the Nile area provide a wide selection of lodgings, ranging from lavish luxury hotels to lovely boutique villas and budget-friendly alternatives. Consider your requirements and interests as you plan your Egyptian vacation, and find the appropriate hotel that will make your travel experience genuinely memorable.

TRAVELING RESOURCES

Whether you're a history buff, an explorer, or just seeking to explore one of the world's most fascinating cities, Cairo and the Nile area provides something for everyone. This chapter will provide useful resources to help you plan and maximize your vacation, such as basic information, lodgings, transportation, attractions, and shopping.

Information In General

Those wishing to visit Cairo and the Nile Valley should remember that Arabic is Egypt's most generally spoken language, although English is extensively used in key tourist areas. The native currency is Egyptian Pounds (EGP). However, hotels and tourist sites accept US dollars, Euros, and credit cards.

Consider visiting travel websites and forums such as TripAdvisor, Lonely Planet, and Travel Egypt to gain advice and suggestions from experienced travelers. Furthermore, local tourist websites such as Experience Egypt and Egypt Travel have up-to-date calendars of events, activities, and festivals you will want to attend.

Accommodations

Cairo has a wide selection of lodgings to fulfill the demands of a wide spectrum of visitors. The Four Seasons, Kempinski, and the historic Marriott Mena House are examples of luxury hotels. Budget visitors will discover a plethora of hostels, guesthouses, and Airbnb listings in the city center and near key attractions.

Consider staying in Luxor or Aswan while seeing the Nile Valley; both offer wonderful ancient temples and sights. Luxor boasts a variety of budget and luxury hotels, including the Sofitel Winter Palace and the Hilton Luxor Resort & Spa. At the same time, Aswan includes quaint Nubian guesthouses and the magnificent Old Cataract Hotel.

Transportation

Getting about Cairo and the Nile area is an exciting journey in and of itself. Several options include local taxis and ridesharing applications like Uber and Careem, the Cairo Metro, public buses, and microbuses (minibusses). Consider a Nile cruise from Cairo to Luxor and Aswan or a deluxe train excursion onboard the Nile Express for a more beautiful experience. Domestic flights from Cairo may also take you to Aswan, Luxor, and other important destinations.

Attractions

Cairo and the Nile region's attractions span millennia and highlight Egypt's rich history and complex culture. Explore classic Cairo landmarks such as the Great Pyramids of Giza, the Sphinx, and the Egyptian Museum, which holds the world's greatest collection of Pharaonic antiquities.

As you go farther down the Nile, don't miss Luxor's ancient temples, particularly the Karnak Temple Complex and the Valley of the Kings, which contains Tutankhamun's tomb. Visit the magnificent Philae Temple, the Unfinished

Obelisk, and the Aswan High Dam while in Aswan.

Consider hiring a local guide or joining a tour group to assist you in exploring these cultural gems. Websites such as GetYourGuide, Viator, and Tripadvisor provide a variety of pre-bookable guided tours and activities.

Shopping

Cairo is a destination for shoppers looking for treasures to take home. Bazaars and markets, like the well-known Khan el-Khalili, offer everything from delicate Egyptian textiles and handmade jewelry to spices, perfumes, and locally manufactured souvenirs. Go to Citystars Mall or Mall of Egypt for high-end shops and international brands. Local souq marketplaces in Luxor and Aswan sell traditional handicrafts, pottery, and Nubian jewelry.

Remember to bargain for the best pricing, have a sense of humor, and be willing to walk away if the offer doesn't seem right.

Visiting Cairo and the Nile is a memorable experience that needs some preparation and planning. Using the variety of online and on-site tools can guarantee that your vacation is all you hoped for and more.

THE TOP TEN MOST LUXURY HOTELS IN CAIRO AND ALONG THE NILE

This chapter highlights ten exceptional hotels that provide well-appointed lodgings and superb service and exhibit Egypt's rich history.

The Four Seasons Hotel Cairo in Nile Plaza is one of the most notable hotels. This exquisite institution in the Garden City neighborhood provides stunning views of the Nile and the metropolis. Guests may pick from exquisite rooms, suites, and top-tier facilities such as a beautiful spa, fine dining restaurants, shops, and a gorgeous terrace pool area.

The Fairmont Nile City, an architectural gem that emanates refinement and grandeur, is not far away. It has large, attractively decorated rooms, exceptional dining experiences, a magnificent rooftop pool area, a cutting-edge spa, and well-equipped meeting facilities. The hotel's closeness to Cairo's central center adds to its allure among discriminating guests.

Another fantastic venue that blends European elegance with true Egyptian charm is the Kempinski Nile Hotel Garden City. This magnificent hotel on the Nile provides beautiful views from its terraces. This hotel is a wonderful choice for an amazing visit due to its distinct dining selections, soothing spa, exclusive cigar lounge, and superb service.

Sofitel Cairo El Gezirah is an oasis in the middle of the city's frantic pace. This 5-star hotel on Gezira Island offers magnificent views of the Nile, the Cairo Tower, and the Pyramids. Guests may choose from various cuisines, including French, Moroccan, and international fare. The infinity pool and the revitalizing SoSpa are ideal for resting after a day of touring the city.

The Marriott Mena House is a historic mansion set on manicured lawns in the shadow of the spectacular Pyramids of Giza. This hotel provides a one-of-a-kind chance to immerse yourself in ancient heritage while still enjoying contemporary conveniences. Luxurious accommodations, exceptional international and regional cuisine, and recreational amenities such as a swimming pool and a golf course add to a memorable vacation.

A trip to Cairo would be completed without a stay at the famed Nile Ritz-Carlton, located in the city's center. Enjoy luxury suites with breathtaking Nile views, a variety of dining choices, an upmarket spa, and spectacular ballrooms. The location of this hotel is ideal for visiting the neighboring Egyptian Museum and Tahrir Square.

The Hilton Cairo Zamalek Residences provides a tranquil refuge in a quiet nook of the busy El Zamalek neighborhood. The hotel's contemporary design has big rooms and suites with private balconies overlooking the Nile. Enjoy a variety of eating options, including the rooftop pool restaurant and a fitness club for a pleasant

CAIRO AND THE NILE TRAVEL GUIDE

break.

The InterContinental Cairo Semiramis is another excellent hotel in the center of Cairo. This business caters to every guest's interests with a comprehensive choice of bedrooms and suites furnished with contemporary and traditional accents. For an abundant well-rounded experience, the hotel also offers outstanding dining choices, a Nile-view pool, and a quiet spa.

With its stunning artwork and modern Thai design, the Dusit Thani LakeView Cairo is the height of refinement for art enthusiasts. The hotel is located in New Cairo's Fifth Settlement and offers large rooms and suites with views of tranquil gardens and a lagoon. Enjoy a variety of world-class dining options, a relaxing spa, and great amenities, making it an ideal location to stay.

Finally, the Steigenberger Hotel El Tahrir is in Cairo's busy central sector. This retreat combines traditional elegance with contemporary comfort and is set near several historical landmarks, retail malls, and eating locations. Guests may unwind in the rooftop pool, which offers spectacular views of Tahrir Square, and choose from various dining choices to suit all tastes.

These top luxury hotels will undoubtedly enrich your stay in Cairo and along the Nile, combining the spirit of Egypt's captivating allure with exceptional service and unique experiences.

10 BEST CAIRO AND NILE ATTRACTIONS AND ACTIVITIES

B rimming with a rich cultural and historical past, these places provide a thrilling mix of world-famous sites and hidden jewels just waiting to be found. Cairo and the Nile provide endless adventure and leisure opportunities, from historic pyramids and mosques to lively markets and charming cruises. Here, we will look at the top 10 sights and activities to assist you in creating a great trip that will leave you with lasting memories.

Begin your journey to the Great Pyramids of Giza.
Every trip to Egypt is complete with seeing the Great Pyramids of Giza, the country's most recognizable emblem. These majestic monuments, set among the desert terrain, have withstood the test of time and continue to astonish visitors from all over the globe. Witness the Great Sphinx's magnificence, and don't pass up the chance to explore the secret chambers of these ancient treasures.

Explore Egyptian history at the Egyptian Museum.
The Egyptian Museum, one of the world's most important archaeological museums, has about 120,000 objects, including ancient mummies, sculptures, jewelry, gilded furniture, and royal chariots. You may better appreciate Egypt's past and marvel at the outstanding quality that has impacted contemporary art and architecture by visiting

this magnificent treasury of ancient history.

Investigate Saladin's Citadel.
The Citadel of Saladin, perched on a limestone hill, provides an intriguing view into Egypt's Islamic past. It was formerly a fortified fortress against invading crusaders, but it today contains the magnificent Muhammad Ali Mosque, the Gawhara Palace, and other important structures. Explore the Citadel's twisting alleyways and take in the panoramic vistas of urban Cairo.

Experience the Kaleidoscope of Khan el-Khalili Bazaar.

Expect sensory overload in the busy Khan el-Khalili Bazaar. This market, a labyrinth of small, maze-like passageways filled with vivid colors and tempting fragrances, provides a one-of-a-kind shopping experience. Bargain through spices, souvenirs, and cutlery, or relax with a sip of traditional mint tea at one of the many coffee shops.

The Whirling Dervishes of Al-Tannoura will captivate you. If you're looking for a genuinely enthralling show, go beyond the Whirling Dervishes of Al-Tannoura. This ancient Sufi dance, accompanied by live music and narrative, will captivate you as performers dressed in colorful clothes move in perfect unison, representing the spiritual essence of the occasion.

Explore the rich history of Old Cairo.
This ancient district, often known as Coptic Cairo, has amazing antiquities from several centuries. Admire the architectural marvels of the Hanging Church and the Ben Ezra Synagogue. A visit to the Coptic Museum, which houses a great collection of ancient art, is a good chance to learn more about the changing cultural history of Old

Cairo.

Admire the Al-Azhar Mosque's Beauty
The Al-Azhar Mosque, built in 972 AD, is a magnificent example of Islamic architecture. As one of the world's oldest institutions, this hallowed monument provides a wealth of historical and cultural insights. Explore its elaborate façade, beautiful minarets, and tranquil courtyards surrounded by lush foliage.

Take a luxurious cruise down the Nile.
Relax on a peaceful Nile River cruise, an important aspect of Egyptian adventure. Enjoy authentic Egyptian food, calming music, and mesmerizing belly dance performances while taking spectacular views of the metropolis. Reserve a felucca ride to soak in the golden colors of the sunset for a romantic experience.

Explore the Imhotep Museum's Journey of Mummification.
The Imhotep Museum, located near the ancient site of Saqqara, houses various remarkable items of Egyptian history. This museum is a must-see for history and archaeology buffs, with displays illustrating the technique and instruments used in mummification and artwork that offers insight into Egypt's architectural evolution.

Feel the Magic of a Hot Air Balloon Ride Fly over Luxor
Glide into the sky of Luxor in a hot air balloon, taking in the breathtaking panoramas of temples, tombs, and ancient ruins. This event will be remembered for a long because of the breathtaking vista of the huge structures lit by the morning sun.

In conclusion, Cairo and the Nile blend history, culture, and natural beauty, offering endless options for an unforgettable adventure. Whether you want adventure, leisure, or spiritual understanding, this enchanted place has something for everyone. So grab your sense of amazement and get ready for an unforgettable Egyptian journey.

TOP 10 DELECTABLE MEALS YOU SHOULD TRY

Travelers going through Cairo and along the Nile will be immersed in Egypt's rich history and unique culture. Indulging in the region's delectable native food is important to this trip. There is no lack of wonderful sensations to captivate your taste buds, from robust meat meals to lovely sweet desserts and tasty vegetarian selections. This chapter introduces you to 10 delectable Egyptian foods you must try.

1. Koshary's

Koshary is a traditional Egyptian dish comprised of rice, pasta, lentils, and chickpeas and topped with crispy onions and garlic tomato sauce. This vegetarian cuisine is excellent and inexpensive, and kosher establishments can be found throughout Cairo. Zooba in Zamalek offers a contemporary touch on this classic for a more premium meal version.

2. Ful Medames

Ful medames is a popular breakfast meal in Cairo, consisting of slow-cooked fava beans blended with olive oil and spices and served with chopped tomatoes and onions. This flavorful lunch, best served with fresh Egyptian bread, will kick-start your day of exploring. Gad, a restaurant franchise with outlets around Cairo, serves the best full mesdames.

3. Shawarma

The iconic Middle Eastern street cuisine shawarma is also a must-try in Egypt. Shawarma, produced locally using marinated beef or chicken, spiced with warm spices, and cooked on a vertical spit, may be packed into sandwiches or served over rice at various restaurants across the city. Al Hamidiyah in Zamalek serves some of Cairo's greatest chicken shawarma.

4. Pigeon Stuffed

The stuffed pigeon, a Nile area specialty, is a sumptuous dish worth trying. Stuffed with rice or freekeh (roasted green wheat), it is grilled or roasted and served with sour molokhia soup. Farahat in the Islamic Cairo area serves generous quantities and delectable flavors.

5. Molokhia

Molokhia is a soup prepared with jute leaves, garlic, and coriander, traditionally eaten with rice, chicken, rabbit, or pigeon. The brilliant green color comes from the healthy plant leaves, while the garlic and coriander provide a spicy and delectable scent. Stop by any typical Egyptian restaurant to eat this flavorful delicacy during your journey.

6. Meats from Egypt - kabab and kofta

Grilled meat dishes are a staple of Egyptian cuisine, and the variety offered will not disappoint. Kabab (grilled skewers of meat) and kofta (grilled minced beef combined with spices) should be on your list of must-try dishes. Treat yourself to various exquisite meat meals at the famed

Kababgy El Azhar, near the Al-Azhar Mosque.

7. Mahshi

Mahshi refers to filled vegetables, including peppers and zucchini, to grape leaves and cabbage. They're often made with rice, onions, and spices and might be vegetarian or include minced meat. Abou Tarek, a restaurant famous for its wonderful selection of stuffed veggies, is a lovely spot to taste mahshi.

8. Sandwich with Alexandrian Liver No. 8

Don't miss out on an Alexandrian liver sandwich, a street food staple famed for spiced liver sautéed with peppers, tomatoes, and onions and served in a warm sandwich for a fascinating voyage of flavors. Look for these tempting sweets from prominent street sellers in Downtown Cairo, such as El Omda or El Gahsh.

9. Falafel from Egypt

Egyptian falafel is a Middle Eastern staple with an Egyptian twist since it uses fava beans instead of chickpeas. This crispy, golden balls of bliss are often served with tahini and lettuce as a filling breakfast or mezze. Zooba has many outlets across Cairo and has some of the greatest falafel in town.

10. Umm Ali

A culinary tour is only complete with a delectable dessert, and Cairo has a fantastic choice in the shape of Umm Ali. Layers of phyllo dough or puff pastry, milk, sugar, and varied nuts are cooked till golden and topped with powdered sugar in this delectable bread pudding. Naguib Mahfouz Café in Khan El Khalili market can satisfy your sweet craving.

You'll experience the wonders of Egypt's gastronomic landscape as you travel Cairo and the Nile area. This list of the top ten tasty delicacies is only the beginning of your savory Egyptian trip.

CONCLUSION

As we near the conclusion of our Cairo and Nile travel guide, it is clear that the area is rich with uncountable treasures and immense beauty that visitors and history buffs cannot afford to miss. Its old attraction and contemporary attractiveness, the rich tapestry of history and culture, and indulgent gastronomic delights make it a memorable vacation. When visiting Cairo and the Nile, one cannot but fall in love with the Egyptians' vivid energy and amicable character, who freely share their tales and secrets with the rest of the world.

Cairo, the huge metropolis born of rich history, not only serves as a gateway to historical treasures but also epitomizes the spirit of a city in motion. Cairo, the Arab world's capital, is known for its beautiful Islamic architecture, enormous marketplaces, vibrant arts sectors, and ever-changing cityscape. The renowned Giza Pyramids, Sphinx, and other significant sites look into the ancient world and demonstrate the might of the Pharaohs.

Egypt's lifeblood, the Nile, is the essential force that has defined its history and future. You may see the ebb and flow of life along its banks and participate in remarkable expeditions to understand the core of Egyptian civilization. Luxor and Aswan, Upper Egypt's crown jewels, should be noticed. They bring visitors back to a realm of heavenly devotion, royal power, and beautiful creativity with their many temples, tombs, and ancient monuments.

A Nile cruise on a luxurious ship or a traditional felucca sailboat leaves you with unforgettable recollections of tranquil landscapes, golden sunsets, and fascinating interactions with local villages.

Egypt's food is an important aspect of the trip, reflecting the country's cosmopolitan heritage and the numerous influences that have influenced Egyptian palates. Cairo and the Nile area provide diverse culinary experiences, from delectable street dishes to opulent fine dining experiences. The colorful cafés, busy markets, and traditional eating businesses offer a lively environment where guests can enjoy delectable foods and local tastes.

Cairo and the Nile area also provide a variety of lodgings to suit any traveler's preferences and budget. Luxurious five-star resorts, charming guesthouses, and family-run boutique hotels dot the landscape, each providing a distinct experience and a true feeling of Egyptian hospitality. Every tourist may discover the ideal spot to call home during their stay among these many housing alternatives.

Throughout this book, we have provided practical recommendations for seeing Cairo and the Nile while addressing important parts of Egyptian culture, traditions, and history. Whether it's about touring the many historical places, keeping safe, shopping for souvenirs, or taking hot air balloon flights, we've given you information that will assist you in planning an amazing trip customized to your specific interests.

As we close the book on this travel guide, we hope it has been informative and motivating, fostering the urge to go on a magnificent voyage to this place of history and magic. Our ultimate goal is to help you develop an intimate relationship with Cairo and the Nile, producing exceptional experiences you will remember for a lifetime. May your voyage to this enthralling place leave an everlasting impression on the pages of your personal history, just as the ancient Egyptians believed in the power of storytelling carved into eternity.

6thJan ⇒ 17th 2023
P/a Easyjet to sphynx airport
1/c BA Cairo main airport
Downtown family Suites
El-Tahrir Squae.

Printed in Great Britain
by Amazon